on track ...

Linda Ronstadt 1969-1989

every album, every song

Daryl Richard Lawrence

sonicbondpublishing.com

Sonicbond Publishing Limited
www.sonicbondpublishing.co.uk
Email: info@sonicbondpublishing.co.uk

First Published in the United Kingdom 2023
First Published in the United States 2023

British Library Cataloguing in Publication Data:
A Catalogue record for this book is available from the British Library

ISBN 978-1-78952-293-8

Typeset in ITC Garamond Std & ITC Avant Garde Gothic
Printed and bound in England

Graphic design and typesetting: Full Moon Media

Follow us on social media:
Twitter: https://twitter.com/SonicbondP
Instagram: www.instagram.com/sonicbondpublishing_/
Facebook: www.facebook.com/SonicbondPublishing/

Linktree QR code:

Acknowledgments

My thanks to Stephen Lambe and the staff at Sonicbond Publishing for indulging my desire to spread the love of Linda Ronstadt's music.

This book is dedicated to my partner, Phillip, as well as the family, friends, acquaintances, colleagues, and total strangers I have regaled with songs and stories from Linda Ronstadt and her career not only during the writing of this book but at many points prior to that as well. Also, a special thanks to our three rabbits Nick, Nora and Asta, who put up with a lot of music (and a lot of repeat listens) in the course of writing this book. I'm sorry if I interrupted your efforts to nap, but I hope the treats made up for it!

Would you like to write for Sonicbond Publishing?

At Sonicbond Publishing we are always on the look-out for authors, particularly for our two main series:

On Track. Mixing fact with in depth analysis, the On Track series examines the work of a particular musical artist or group. All genres are considered from easy listening and jazz to 60s soul to 90s pop, via rock and metal.

On Screen. This series looks at the world of film and television. Subjects considered include directors, actors and writers, as well as entire television and film series. As with the On Track series, we balance fact with analysis.

While professional writing experience would, of course, be an advantage the most important qualification is to have real enthusiasm and knowledge of your subject. First-time authors are welcomed, but the ability to write well in English is essential.

Sonicbond Publishing has distribution throughout Europe and North America, and all books are also published in E-book form. Authors will be paid a royalty based on sales of their book.

Further details are available from www.sonicbondpublishing.co.uk. To contact us, complete the contact form there or email info@sonicbondpublishing.co.uk

on track ...

Linda Ronstadt

1969-1989

Contents

Introduction

Linda Ronstadt, born in Tucson, Arizona on 15 July 1946, started appreciating music practically from the moment of her birth and was exposed to many different genres of music growing up, which may well have informed her career trajectory later in life. After graduating from high school, she moved out to Los Angeles to be a singer. Once she had arrived, she formed The Stone Poneys with Kenny Edwards and Bobby Kimmel; she had known Kimmel for some years and it was a desire to form a band with him that informed her move to Los Angeles. Kimmel had met Edwards while living in L.A. and the three of them decided to make a go of it, but aside from 'Different Drum', the group did not find success. The band were a folk rock band and struggled to find their niche and sound. The release of 'Different Drum' in its final recorded form was, ultimately, the high point and the beginning of the end for the group. Originally conceived and performed as a folksy tune, it morphed into a baroque pop behemoth that left Ronstadt's bandmates on the side, as she laid down lead vocals in front of an orchestra. The record label saw her potential as a solo act and the rest, as they say, is history. Henry Diltz, the famed rock photographer, described her in her Stone Poney days as 'barefoot all the time, a real country girl' in a presentation that the author attended in August 2023.

Throughout this book, you'll read about 17 albums Ronstadt released after her solo career began in 1969. There's really an album for everyone contained within these 17, as they vary from country, country-rock, rock and pop, to jazz and mariachi. The adventurous listener can even get a taste of operetta if they feel like it. The influences of her childhood showed Ronstadt that musical appeal can be found across genres and, even within the same genre, different types of material.

After a rocky start to her solo career, Ronstadt took off in the mid-1970s and never looked back. Along with shattering many records for female singers, she also created a role for women in the industry by taking control of her career. Not satisfied with being typecast as one sort of singer, she eventually collected enough credibility in the music industry to do whatever she wanted. While she made those moves on the business side of things, she also continued to improve and refine her own singing abilities, allowing her to interpret a broad range of material. By the end of the two decades profiled in this book, she was able to take any song at all and make it her own. Awards never meant much to Ronstadt, although she collected many. It was her ability to choose her own material and sing it that brought her true joy.

So, how should you utilize this book? Well, there are one of two ways. The first, for those very familiar with Ronstadt's material, is to use it to revisit some of those songs you may not have listened to in a while. Song meanings change with time and their ability to elicit different feelings and emotions adapt to someone's circumstances. For those not as familiar with some parts of the Ronstadt catalog, this book can serve as a roadmap. It gives the reader a taste of what a song may mean, but then it is up to them to listen and see how it impacts them. In either case, treat it as a roadmap. While every song may not resonate, the least you can do is give it a chance.

Hand Sown...Home Grown (1969)

Personnel:
Linda Ronstadt: vocals, finger cymbals
Ken Edwards: acoustic guitar
Pete Childs: acoustic guitar
Bob Kimmel: acoustic guitar
Cyrus Faryar: acoustic guitar, bouzouki
John T. Forsha: acoustic guitar, electric guitar
Jimmy Bond: bass
Billy Mundi: drums
Clarence White: electric guitar
Red Rhodes: pedal steel guitar
Produced in Los Angeles in 1969 by Chip Douglas
Release date: 1969
Running time: 31:50

The first solo album from Linda Ronstadt had high expectations. The woman who had made 'Different Drum' a hit record had a strong voice and an even stronger ambition to make it as a singer. Ronstadt's solo appeal was made apparent to her Stone Poneys bandmates even as they began their work together, as Herb Cohen said that he would be able to get her a deal, but he wasn't sure about the package deal, including the band. Even at that early juncture in her career, Ronstadt knew she had something that set her apart and above being in a group. Despite this, the Stone Poneys recorded three albums together, although the last was titled *Linda Ronstadt, Stone Poneys and Friends, Vol. III*. The writing was on the wall and the band broke up after that. 'No boost to band morale, it was the beginning of the end of the Stone Poneys', wrote Ronstadt in her memoirs about that album. In a 1969 article for *Fusion*, Ronstadt was even blunter, 'And that was the end of it, man. The beginning of the end. Which, really, didn't bother me that much 'cause that group was really more of a learning experience than anything else'.

Capitol's contract with Ronstadt was predatory, especially after her Poneys bandmates were taken off the accounting books. The money spent on producing the Stone Poney albums was assumed solely by Linda and her subsequent solo recordings only deepened that debt. 'It would be eight years before I would see any money from record sales', wrote Linda. Thus, we are at the beginning of her journey to both solo success and financial solvency with this album.

The album itself was a flop. It sold less than 10,000 copies before the follow-up album came out, which is horrifying in retrospect when you look at what her later albums would sell. The strength of her name was not enough to carry an album and although 'Different Drum' was recognizable, it wasn't enough for an entire record to be sold on reputation alone. As the *Linda Ronstadt Scrapbook* boldly put it, 'Linda's first solo album *Hand Sown...Home Grown* lacked cohesiveness and response'. This is a very polite way of saying that it didn't live up to fans' expectations due to both the track selection and the way in which it was received by critics and the general public.

Making the album was also a strain, as manager Herb Cohen and Linda did not get along and did not have a shared vision of her career. Linda sat down for an interview with *Country Music People* in 1977 and reflected on the creation of this album.

> Every session was an argument – we didn't get along too well, although he's very nice, and I think he's a pretty good producer. Ultimately, whenever I complain about something that's gone down on my records, I always end up with only myself to blame, because no matter how good your ideas are, and how much feeling you have and want to communicate, until you develop your craft and can use it, it doesn't do any good.

Ronstadt, while shifting the blame to herself, also illuminated the fact that conditions have to be right for true creativity to flourish – and an adversarial manager relationship was not conducive to a great overall product.

Ronstadt was even harder on herself in 1971 when the failure of this album was still very fresh. Chatting with Robert Windeler from *Stereo Review*, Linda was honest about the album and its lack of success:

> All the discipline in this country is one person to another: parents spanking, a teacher or coach always on your back. But nobody teaches us how to discipline ourselves. We have no bloody security, we're emotional weaklings, easy to brainwash; it's easy to get our attention for a while with any new trend. Nobody learned a thing from the Manson trial, for instance. Those were really lame chicks, looking for somebody to tell them what to do, and there are a lot of that kind of people around.

Linda, here, doubled down on work ethic and would steadily pour more and more time into learning not only the music side of the business – by spending more time in the booth – but on the business side as well, seeing what did, didn't and could work. Although this album was not the charting success she may have hoped for, it was a success in guiding her career and forming the mind of the formidable artist she would become.

'Baby You've Been On My Mind' (Dylan)

Linda opens this album with a cover of a Bob Dylan song, showing she still had one foot in the folk scene as she embarked on her solo career. While the album cover may have been slightly country-tinged, this song is definitely something that could have easily been a Stone Poneys cut instead of one from her solo career. It's an upbeat piano-driven song that glistens with late-60s flavor and is a good selection to kick off the album. There's even a Beatles-esque horn solo in the middle of the song to remind the listener firmly of where they are in pop music history. The production on the song is expansive and lush, leaving the listener to wonder why it wasn't released as a single – it certainly had the potential to at least chart, even if it may not have climbed to the top.

A promotional film was made for this song, filmed for an episode of the short-lived variety show called *Something Else* hosted by John Byner. It opened with Linda tossing around a Frisbee on the beach with Byner. The film then morphs into Ronstadt singing the song, dressed in a white top and shorts, on the same beach. The footage of the waves splashing against the shore underscores the longing lyrics sung by Linda as she walks and contemplates the object of her affection. The video ends with Ronstadt apologizing to Byner for breaking into song, then resuming their Frisbee tossing. It's a charming example of Ronstadt's playfulness as a performer early in her career and how casually she took her image at this early stage.

'Silver Threads And Golden Needles' (Reynolds/Rhodes)

The first of two versions released by Ronstadt on her early albums, this track is less country and more pop than its successor a few years later. While there is pedal steel guitar on the track, it is buried in the mix and the whole song is more acoustically based than the later version. The arrangement on this song is the less popular of the two Linda released and, overall, she is not given much of a chance to let her voice break free of the instrumentation on the song. This may have been the primary motivator for her to revisit the song later, a practice she didn't do except on this occasion. While this is certainly a good track for the album, it wasn't the standout its later version was and Ronstadt would probably like people to overlook this version.

'Bet No One Ever Hurt This Bad' (Newman)

This track presents a rarity for Ronstadt as she infrequently ever turned to Randy Newman for a tune. In fact, this is only one of two times she ever recorded a song written by the prolific Newman. The song is funky, with the guitar twang and drum work serving to shape the song's feel around Ronstadt's narrative. The guitar work itself feels country western initially, before setting itself into more of a groove as the song progresses, and the addition of an organ helps to fill out the track. The tempo changes between the verses and chorus, with Ronstadt able to show off both quick and slow vocals that highlight her ability to weave within the structure of any song. Linda's come-hither lyrics are hypnotizing against the backdrop of the full band put together for this recording and it's a fun hidden gem waiting for listeners to discover.

'A Number And A Name' (Campbell/Gillette)
Linda, accompanied by folksy acoustic guitar, builds this song with vocals that are reminiscent of 'Different Drum'. As the song progresses, more instruments are layered in, including a string section and an organ. The smooth song sails out of the speakers as Ronstadt sings the listener through the story of her lost love. A proficient interpreter of heartbreak from the outset of her career, Linda tunes into particular emotions and is able to draw them out of those who invest time and money in her albums. Her most successful songs, especially in the pop music realm, deal with heartbreak and sorrow in a relatable way that ooze emotion, making even the saddest lyrics come to life. The feel of the album has been established by this time and Ronstadt's way with songs has been keyed in. This track, although low-key and mellow, is indicative of the material Ronstadt and her producer picked for this album in order to capitalize on her Stone Poneys success.

'Only Mama That'll Walk The Line' (Bryant)
This song, made most famous by Waylon Jennings the year prior to this album, gave Linda a chance to interpret a song solidly in the country music realm. Ronstadt changed the gender from the original version and ran away with the track from that point. It's an upbeat tune that Linda growls her way through to emphasize some of the lyrics, giving a different texture to this track, which contrasts with others that feature entirely smooth vocalizations from her. While definitely country, Ronstadt was able to inject a little funk into the track and made it bop along with her delivery of the lyrics.

Although Jennings released the song in 1968, Ronstadt was the first person to perform it on Johnny Cash's variety show; Jennings would perform it the following year on the same show. Appearing on a soundstage decorated with various props evoking the American West, Ronstadt sings the song wearing a purple-striped minidress and with an amazing amount of hair piled up on her head.

'The Long Way Around' (Edwards)
This track was the only song released as a single to promote the album; it didn't chart until early 1971 and, at that point, it only rose to number 70. This song was written by Linda's former bandmate in the Stoney Poneys, Kenny Edwards, whose lyrics about young love spoke to Ronstadt's affection for such material. The song's arrangement is typical of pop music for the time, including a piano and soft drumming. The most surprising aspect of the song is the inclusion of a string section, as the song's arrangement doesn't necessarily need it. However, 'Different Drum' was known for lush orchestration and the desire to replicate that song's success may have driven the decision to add something along those lines, especially when it was identified as single material for the wider listening audience.

'Break My Mind' (Loudermilk)

This song, which opens the second side of the album, is more country than the material that had come before. The prominent use of the steel guitar on the track is responsible for this and, in combination with the electric guitar work, makes it sound like something from an album or two later down the line (in truth, it is more country rock than some tracks on later albums that purported to be entirely country rock). Linda is able to wield her voice as a southern-inspired weapon and have her way with this jam of a track.

Ronstadt performed this song on the television show *It's Happening* in 1969 and, against a backdrop of neon-colored versions of her picture from the album cover, gets into the groove of the track and sways along while delivering her vocals. Those vocals skew more towards Janis Joplin than country on this show, which had live vocals instead of a prerecorded track that other shows utilized at the time.

'I'll Be Your Baby Tonight' (Dylan)

In a sign of the times, Linda turned to her second Bob Dylan song for the album. The slower tune was the space Ronstadt needed to stretch out her notes and let her vocals take control, with minimal interference from the backing band. At times, the fiddle playing alongside her seems more like a duet partner than a competing musical influence. The listener can float along and follow the song thanks to Ronstadt's smooth vocal delivery. Ronstadt's arrangement of the song differed enough from Dylan's to make it unique; while Dylan's version was very folk, Linda's skewed more towards country.

'It's About Time' (Douglas)

This song, right in the middle of the second side of the album, holds the course for the mellow feeling. It straddles several genres, including folk, pop and country, therefore, successfully predicting the failure of the music industry to categorize her for the first part of her solo career. The song is executed well, but Capitol didn't know how to market the specific type of music Ronstadt favored with her interpretations. This song, in short, is an example of Capitol's self-imposed nightmare: how do you market an extremely versatile and capable singer who refuses to commit to one genre? This particular song glides smoothly across the vinyl and succeeds in keeping a cohesive sound for Linda to play with. While not the most vocally demanding song, it was able to give her a chance to sing a song that would please listeners nonetheless.

'We Need A Whole Lot More Of Jesus (And A Lot Less Rock & Roll)' (Raney)

This may be the longest song title in Linda Ronstadt's entire catalog and is her interpretation of a song first released a decade prior. While it was originally intended as a critique of rock music, by the time Linda sang it, the song had become a way of lampooning critics of the genre by turning their own lyrics around at them. Linda's version is the most well-known interpretation of the song and, thus, is the most widely accepted. The way in which Linda and her fellow artists in the late 60s were able to take such a song and weaponize it against their critics is something that she rarely had the opportunity to do. This track is a good example of how, early in her career, she was able to make statements through music that would be stymied later on.

'The Dolphins' (Neil)

For the last track on the album, Ronstadt turned to a folk tune written by Fred Neil (whose best-known composition may be 'Everybody's Talking', made famous by Harry Nilsson). The message of this song, of love and peace, is very much an element of its time and is best understood in the context of the larger musical and cultural scene as it existed in 1969. It's an effective song that was her contribution to rallying folks to understand and love one another. The guitar work on the track gives it a wavy, aquatic feel as Linda sings about her search for dolphins in the sea, a clever way of saying she is trying to find the peace she and the world need. However, as the song's narrator, she also admits that she isn't the one to tell the world what to do. The slippery slope of popular music becoming a rallying point of activism had mixed results and while Ronstadt espoused peace in the song, she doesn't go so far as putting herself out there as someone who could enact change with a song.

Bonus Track

'(She's A) Very Lovely Woman' (Rhodes)

Technically, this song was the single released from the album, although its B-side of 'The Long Way Around' was the song that was pushed by the record company as the single. It, along with its flip side, didn't chart until over a year after this album was released. As a non-album track, this song existed in the ether until it was finally released in a 2009 compilation; prior to that, the only way to listen to it was on the 45.

A dramatic song with a funky groove, it gave Ronstadt the opportunity to utilize her big vocals alongside her quiet, almost whispering vocals. The range of her voice is on full display here, showcasing what she is capable of. Ronstadt performed this song on Andy Williams' variety show, giving a rare glimpse into how she performed material from this time in her career.

Silk Purse (1970)

Personnel:
Linda Ronstadt: vocals
Musician credits were not included on this album
Produced at Cinderella Sound, Nashville and Woodland Sound Studios between 5 January 1970 and 4 March 1970 by Elliot F. Mazer
Release date: 13 April 1970
Highest chart place: US: 103
Running time: 29:14

Linda Ronstadt's sophomore album provided her with the opportunity to grow as an artist and record a mix of folk, country and pop songs. Like a buffet, it is varied and full of choices for listeners to enjoy. In retrospect, the album is known for two things: the song 'Long, Long Time' and the album cover itself.

As reported in *Circus* magazine in May 1970, 'The title of the album was arrived at after the photo session. Linda got the pig idea partly to keep her country image and partly because – well, she likes pigs'. As Linda told the author of the article Phil Morris, 'I tried to feed one a ham sandwich and he wouldn't eat it. I was so proud of him'. After trying out a number of pork-related titles, Linda and the record company settled on *Silk Purse* due to the common saying, 'You can't make a silk purse out of a sow's ear'. Linda herself explained a bit more about the album cover in her memoir, saying the decision to take the photo in a pig pen was an ironic statement regarding whether she and her peers should be good earth wives and mothers and stay at home or give space to themselves to have the freedom to be 'funky mamas' who could hang with the guys at places like the Troubadour. The inspiration for the way she dressed and posed came from Moonbeam McSwine, a character from the *Li'l Abner* comic strip she read in the local paper back home in Arizona. 'I got away with more of my ideas than a lot of people did', she shared with Jeff Kahliss of the Alta Journal while reflecting on the album cover.

The back cover of the record tried very hard to sell Ronstadt as a serious artist, comparing her skills to Bob Dylan, Billie Holiday, Edith Piaf, Jerry Lee Lewis, Hank Williams and Johnny Cash. If a bit was taken from each of these and put into a blender, the result, they said, would be Linda Ronstadt. In a touch straight out of 1970, they even lean into the concept of reincarnation and say that 'within her [is] the force, the power of all that is music...' Capitol had no clue how to sell her as an artist and grasped at anything they could to appeal to the masses. The liner notes are sparse and credits are hard to come by for some aspects of the album; there is still a mystery surrounding who even took the iconic photograph for the cover.

In an interview with *Country Music Roundup*, Linda was glib about what was contained on the record: 'It has songs on it with words and melody. I don't know, it's kinda hard to talk about it'. In answer to a question about if she wanted to be a superstar, Linda said:

> I think it would be real nice. I just moved into a new house and I have a lot of rent to pay and I think it would be nice if I could just manage to pay the rent. Until such time when society's completely falling apart and money's no longer of any use to anyone.

Even at this early stage of her career, she showcased a sense of humor and a social awareness that would be more on display once she was an established powerhouse in the music industry.

Overall, Ronstadt didn't remember this album fondly. In a 1975 interview with *Rolling Stone*, Linda told Ben Fong-Torres, 'I hate that album', and was further described as 'easily forgettable' by her. 'I couldn't sing then, I didn't know what I was doing. I was working with Nashville musicians and I don't really play country music; I very definitely play California music, and I couldn't communicate it to them'.

Despite her feelings on the album as her career progressed, this is a foundational record of how she developed as an artist. While Linda would have been a superstar without this record, it would have taken longer. Through the creative process of this album, she discovered that country wasn't her preferred genre. Instead, country rock would be her driving creative passion for the next few years. As opposed to the influence of Nashville, leaning more heavily on California influences would lead her to create magic in the studio and on stage. In less than half an hour (the running time of the album), she creates a statement for herself and her future.

'Lovesick Blues' (Friend/Mills)

Arranged and conducted by Kenneth Buttrey

Although this song originated in the early 1920s as a Tinpan Alley song, which made its way into a musical, it didn't catch on as a country song until Hank Williams performed it on the *Louisiana Hayride* radio show. The public loved his version of the song so much that he cut a record of it, whereupon it rocketed to the top of the *Billboard* Country & Western chart shortly after its February 1949 release. Eventually, after being named the top song of the year by a couple of different organizations, it became the biggest hit of Hank Williams' career.

Prior to Ronstadt recording it, the most recent popular iteration of the song was sung by Frank Ifield and released in 1962, where it quickly gained popularity. Therefore, there was a span of almost a decade before Linda decided to interpret this song for herself to lead off her second solo album. Linda's version is upbeat and features her pseudo-yodeling on some of the notes to emphasize them. It's a pretty traditional country arrangement and she's backed by a proficient band that are able to evoke the twang Ronstadt's voice lacks. It's a great introduction to the rest of the album and gets the listener in the mood to continue onto the next track. Linda's version almost made it a bit of a mod interpretation; adding a rock sensibility transformed it from something familiar into something fun and bouncy, appealing to the fans of her Stone Poneys days and helping to grow her solo fanbase.

Ronstadt sang this track during a performance on *Playboy After Dark*, in which she is dressed in a floral pattern mini dress. As the crowd grooved around her, she stood and crooned the song to the assembled partygoers. The purpose of this show was to make a viewer seem like they were right in the middle of a good time and Ronstadt did everything she could to create that atmosphere. Before music videos, appearances such as these served as a way for artists to promote their latest record. There's also an audio recording of a live performance of this song from Big Sur in 1970, which showed that Linda could speed up the tempo of the song and make it a real barnburner of a number. This performance strips away some of the song's country sound, leaving it as a traditional country rock song that would be more of her go-to genre for the next few years.

Mary Ellen Moore, writing about this song several years later, admitted that this version couldn't outshine Hank Williams', but 'Linda's version is excellent and is a perfect example of the heights she could reach when she really tried'.

'Are My Thoughts With You?' (Newbury)
Arranged and conducted by Elliot Mazer and Adam Mitchell
For the next track, Ronstadt chose to slow it down and weave a meaningful organ into the background of the song. Linda's vocals are strong from the start and a lonesome harmonica part joins her in telling the mournful tale of the song. The backing vocals help underscore the emotions Ronstadt strives to make the listener feel. This was a relatively new song, only coming out in 1968 on the first album released by its writer, Mickey Newbury. Newbury would go on to become one of the best-known songwriters in the country scene, so selecting this song showed Ronstadt's knack for recognizing good material and reinterpreting it.

This was the height of Ronstadt appearing on television to support her albums. She was still fresh in people's minds from her Stone Poney days and there were plenty of variety programs, especially in the country genre, that needed new material for their episodes. It is no surprise, then, that Ronstadt was also given an opportunity to trot this song out for a television performance. Crooning from a set made to look like the front of a middle America home, Ronstadt stands on the porch and belts out this torch song with no visible band. Dressed in the same mini dress, with long peasant sleeves more prominent, Linda is the picture of a lovely, young, heartbroken singer. It's obvious this was sung for a taping, as the audience clapping is piped in while Ronstadt is still singing the song. However, this version differed from the album version; there's no lip-syncing involved on Ronstadt's part, although she may have been singing along to a taped band performance.

'Will You Love Me Tomorrow' (Goffin/King)
Arranged and conducted by Elliot Mazer and Adam Mitchell
It's funny to think that Ronstadt's version of this song came out a mere nine years after the version recorded by the Shirelles, but the gulf of the 1960s and its decade of upheaval stands between the two versions. This is Ronstadt's only recorded interpretation of a Goffin-King composition. Carole King, of course, was well-established as a songwriter in her own right and would explode onto the music scene as a singer shortly after this album's release with her landmark *Tapestry* album. The record company released Ronstadt's version as the lead single from this album on 2 March 1970. The use of a recognizable song to drum up excitement for the forthcoming album, which came out in April, was a canny tactic to drive album sales. While the single didn't break the Top 100 on the *Billboard* chart, it is still a notable version of the song that holds the distinction of being the last released before King's own version.

Ronstadt's interpretation is more rocking than either of the preceding tracks on the album. Although it retains a tinge of country, the arrangement is undoubtedly poppier than the listener would have been used to thus far in the album or, perhaps, her entire solo career leading up to this track. It's debatable if backing vocals are needed for Linda's interpretation of this song, as they can either be seen as an asset or a distraction from her lead vocals. They do add a punch, but the punch may not be entirely necessary.

As promotion for the album started to heat up, Linda appeared on *The Johnny Cash Show* a week after the single's release to sing it live. The country superstar had his own show and invited Linda on to promote the song. For the performance, Ronstadt wore the same dress she did for the two prior taped performances. Ronstadt didn't have a large budget and the record company wouldn't have invested any money in her wardrobe, so it was up to her to focus the audience on her vocal performance and, hopefully, not notice her lack of variety in clothes. Again, Linda is the only one on stage for the performance, and the instrumental and backing vocal tracks, at least, seem lifted right from the album. Just as the record company got her out of the Stone Poneys so she could be the sole focus, they kept anyone else but Ronstadt from appearing onstage in support of the song and album. After all, it was Linda on the album cover – with a couple of pigs.

'Nobody's' (White)
Arranged and conducted by Norbert Putnam and Adam Mitchell
On the same day the lead single for the album was released, Ronstadt was in the studio recording this song for the first side of the album. This highlights

the incredibly tight turnaround between Linda laying down the tracks and the album being cut and released. Capitol obviously wanted to pump this album out quickly, which left little room for error in the recording process.

In contrast to the prior song, the backing vocals add so much to Linda's interpretation of this song. The choir atmosphere they create combines with an arrangement that seems like it belongs on one of her albums at least five years in the future. This song, more than any other so far on the album, shows Ronstadt's potential for arranging a song and having it produced to showcase her talents, as well as fill a track with a wall of sound that lends it fullness. In fact, without the harmonica, this song could have easily been placed on an album like *Prisoner In Disguise* and no one would have known it was recorded five years before. It really is a tantalizing window into her future and seems like a Peter Asher production, even though he was nowhere near this album and wouldn't come into the picture as a producer for Ronstadt for another three years.

'Louise' (Siebel)

Guest musician – Gary White

Before Bonnie Raitt covered this song written by Paul Siebel, Linda was able to record her version of it and get it out seven years before the fiery redhead released hers. Ronstadt chose this song to end the first side of her album and, thus, close out one experience and prepare listeners for another as they flipped the vinyl over. Linda chose to record this song as a duet with Gary White, who harmonized with Ronstadt's lead vocals and provided depth to the vocal performance overall. Phil Morris, in *Circus*, described the song bluntly as 'the life story of a truck-stop whore'.

The arrangement for the song is rather simple, with just an acoustic guitar accompanying Ronstadt and White. The track features a strong country vocal from Linda, who again switched to an almost-yodel for her high notes. There's a sweetness and richness to her voice as she sings about a rather unfortunate woman. The choice of this song as a way to close out side one is extremely effective, as it leaves the listener wanting more after hearing about Louise's fate. It's a subdued, stripped-down performance that resonates and when the needle moves past the grooves, there's no other choice but to continue onto side two. Linda's version of the song was so simple and effective that Raitt's arrangement was very similar for her version on *Sweet Forgiveness*.

Morris described the recording of the song, which is somewhat the opposite of the song immediately following it on the record:

> Linda had wanted to record the tune since first hearing it, but she wasn't sure she could sing it well. The way it came to be on the record was when she and Gary White and Elliot [Mazer, the producer on the record] and some others were in the studio doing preliminary demos for the album.

> They had worked hard and, at about three in the morning, everyone was exhausted and had their coats on – ready to leave. Linda sat back on the console in the control room and 'Louise' just started rolling out. Gary said, 'Let's do it', and he grabbed a guitar and they went out into the studio and did one take with Gary on guitar and singing harmony. Elliot leaned back in his chair and fell asleep and they didn't even listen to the take until several days later. When they did it, it was right there; the song was just there, even though it had only been a demo. And that's the track that will be used on the album.

'Long, Long Time' (White)
Arranged and conducted by Norbert Putnam
As early as 1985, this song was regarded as not only a classic but a song that epitomized ultimate sadness. In an Esquire article that describes the song as already having a cult following, Linda told the interviewer Ron Rosenbaum that multiple actors had told her they played the song right before sad scenes to get them in the right headspace. Regarding the narrator of the song, Rosenbaum asks if the love is unconsummated. After trying to toss the question aside, Ronstadt provides a glimpse into how she internalized this song and based her performance on a real relationship – with a married man who, indeed, she slept with.

'I can remember the day I recorded 'Long, Long Time'', Linda told Rosenbaum.

> It was 10:30 in the morning, but I was really into this kind of achy feeling because the music – it's in these chords. I think my phrasing was horrible. I think I kind of butchered it, but it is definitely in those chords. And it happened to the musicians, who are jaded session players. As soon as the fiddle player and Weldon Myrick, who's the steel guitar, began to play those chords, they got real into that and became personally involved ...

In the liner notes to a compilation of her Capitol records, music journalist Barry Alfonso reports that Ronstadt fell asleep in the studio's control room after the second take of the song due to the energy she exerted in belting out the song.

The genius of the song was recognized by *Circus* magazine in May 1970, where Phil Morris wrote that it was '...about a girl who has become withdrawn and can't handle it anymore. You have to hear the whole song. It just could become a classic'. At the time Morris wrote the article, the album would have just come out ahead of his deadline for the May issue.

Linda, in her memoir, recalled the first time she heard the song performed by its writer Gary White after a show he played with Paul Siebel at the Café Au Go-Go. He took his guitar out and played it for her and she immediately laid claim to the privilege of recording it. 'I never liked my performance on the record', Ronstadt said. 'It was recorded at ten in the morning, somewhat early for a singer, and we used the live vocal. I learned to sing it better later. It was a big hit for me in 1970, and it bought me time to learn'.

Describing it as 'a big hit' is underselling the impact it had on Ronstadt's career. It was her first hit and brought national attention to her burgeoning solo career. It reached number 25 on the *Billboard* Hot 100 and earned her a Grammy nomination for the 1971 awards. The song gained steam throughout the summer, having been released as the second and final single from the album in May 1970. Capitol finally listened to her pleas and released it as a single, as Linda told *Rolling Stone* in 1975, but was told to never ask them to release a country single again.

Guitarist John Beland, who joined Ronstadt's band shortly after the release of the album, described, in his memoir, watching Ronstadt rehearse the song before a performance on the Everly Brothers' variety show. 'When Linda sang 'Long, Long Time', you couldn't help but get goosebumps all over'. Ronstadt performed this song on many shows over the next few years; first, in support of the album, then later, as the song she was most recognized for before her true breakthrough album in 1974.

Since its release, it has been used in television and movies to elicit an emotional reaction from viewers, even being featured in the dystopian fantasy series *The Last Of Us* in 2023. Interest in the song is evergreen and provides one of several entry points for new listeners to discover Linda Ronstadt. It is also the earliest song that may be widely appealing from her catalog, as the other songs on the shortlist, such as 'You're No Good', 'Blue Bayou' and 'When Will I Be Loved', come from her mid-70s pop heyday.

Linda herself, however, revealed in a 2020 interview with *Mix Online* how she feels about the song. When asked if she ever gets a chill when listening to the song, she responded:

> A chill of disgust. I hadn't learned the phrasing yet. I needed to learn it on my guitar first, and I didn't have time to do that before we recorded it. There are some live versions that are a little better. Listen, some things are better than others.

'Mental Revenge' (Tillis)

Mel Tillis, a member of the outlaw country community in the 1970s that pushed country music beyond its confined, conservative limits, penned this song. This song announces its arrival with a strong fiddle part and seems more traditional country than something that pushes any limits, as Mel Tillis wrote this song before outlaw country was around. After the crashing start, the song slows in tempo as Linda croons about taking sweet mental revenge on a man who has done her wrong. The song continues this way throughout, with the verses speeding by with the help of the punchy fiddle before slowing down to a languorous speed for the chorus.

The song is a fun ditty about the singer being wronged and the many ways in which her former lover can be made to pay for everything they did. This song, in particular, may have had the heaviest load to carry on the album, coming after 'Long, Long Time' and its orchestral sound. As with many of Ronstadt's albums (a prime example is *Hasten Down the Wind*), the type of song changed with each track. This track is more energetic and spunky compared to the previous track, thus not allowing a string of similar songs to set the mood for an entire album side. While it is not as memorable as the previous song on the album, it serves as a transition from a hit single to the rest of the album side and, at the very least, intrigues the listener about what might be ahead.

'I'm Leaving It Up to You' (Harris/Terry)

Linda Ronstadt's interpretation of this song has the unenviable position of being stuck on the second side of her record but also sandwiched between two better-known versions of the same song: the original by Dale & Grace released in 1962, and the best-known cover released in 1974 by Donny & Marie. Ronstadt's version varies in a couple of significant ways, however, that make it worth a listener's time.

First, it puts a country spin on a doo-wop classic; by adding country instrumental elements, it is given a fresh sound. Second, vocal duties are handled by only one person. With Linda singing the part and not performing it as a duet, she takes a calculated chance in making this song a solo number without the need for a partner to do the vocal lifting with her. Her voice is more than capable of pulling it off and the reward is a fun revisit of a song that was almost a decade old within the pop culture zeitgeist at the time.

Ronstadt taking this song also drew it out of pre-Beatles obscurity to give it another chance at success. The better-known 70s version was still years away, giving Linda the distinction of keeping the tune in the public eye. In some ways, culture moved at a faster pace in this era than it currently does, as songs were constantly revised and refreshed. Even at less than a decade old, a song such as this would be considered old and ripe for interpretation.

'He Dark The Sun' (Clark/Leadon)

The most remarkable part of this track, of course, is Ronstadt's powerful vocals. The final version on the album starts with vocals from Linda before an acoustic guitar enters to form an accompaniment. This song was intended as a showcase for her voice and by giving it primacy within the arrangement, it's undeniable this song belongs solely to Ronstadt's voice. This is the type of song that sounds like it was specifically crafted entirely and only for her interpretation and, indeed, her version of the Bernie Leadon and Gene Clark song is the one most widely known and available to hear.

The song, which is also known as 'He Darked The Sun', has an alternate version that was included on the compilation album *The Best of Linda*

Ronstadt: The Capitol Years released in 2006. This is the only bonus track relating to Silk Purse and gives listeners a chance to hear what an amped-up country version of the song sounded like. There is a lot more fiddle and the track feels much more downhome than the version released on the album. There is also a difference in delivery and tone, as the final album version begins on a much more ominous note, with Ronstadt launching into the end of the chorus 'and with the length of his mind/he dark the sun'. The alternate take, meanders up to the chorus and builds the story of the song before it gets to the dark chorus. It's a small but significant storytelling change that makes a large difference to the tone and feel of the overall track. On this alternate track, Ronstadt's vocals are more buried in the arrangement and we see what could have been, but luckily wasn't to be, with the release of this song.

'Life Is Like A Mountain Railway' (traditional)
Arranged by Elliott Mazer and Linda Ronstadt
Guest musicians – The Beechwood Rangers
This is the song with the longest history on the album, originating in the prior century as a musical interpretation of a poem, which transformed into a hymn. At the time, country music was still heavily influenced by Christian imagery, so it's no surprise that a hymn-based song made it onto what was, primarily, a country album. A veritable who's who in country music had recorded versions of the song, so it was quite familiar to listeners at the time.

Ronstadt's interpretation of the song takes the listener to church, as she is backed by a significant choir of voices to make this track the most traditional-sounding offering on the entire album. Relying upon her voice to break through the chorus behind her, she ably steers the listener through its slow tempo. Her solo in the middle of the song, underscored by the crooning of the background singers, gives her a chance to break away from the rest and carry the story towards its conclusion. It's a very lowkey way of ending the album, in contrast to albums later this decade, where the last song was reserved for Ronstadt to do something outside the norm from the rest of the album. This track bookends a country experience that, with some deviation, stayed close to that genre throughout.

Linda Ronstadt (1972)

Personnel:
Linda Ronstadt: lead vocals, arrangements, tambourine
Barry Beckett: keyboards
John Boylan: guitar, arrangements
Glenn Frey: guitar, arrangements, backing vocals
"Sneaky" Pete Kleinow: pedal steel guitar
Richard Bowden: electric guitar
Tippy Armstrong: guitar
Weldon Myrick: steel guitar
Bernie Leadon: guitar, backing vocals
Herb Pedersen: guitar, backing vocals, banjo
Dean Webb: mandolin
Moon Martin: backing vocals, guitar
Buddy Emmons: pedal steel guitar
Michael Bowden: bass guitar
David Hood: bass guitar
Wesley Pritchett: bass guitar
Randy Meisner: bass guitar, backing vocals
Lyle Ritz: bass guitar
Don Henley: drums, backing vocals
Roger Hawkins: drums
Mike Botts: drums
Jimmie Fadden: harmonica
Gib Guilbeau: fiddle, backing vocals
J. D. Souther: backing vocals, lead and harmony vocals
Merry Clayton, Dianne Davidson, Miss Ona: backing vocals
Produced at United Western, Hollywood, The Troubadour, Hollywood and Muscle Shoals, Sheffield, Alabama in 1971 by John Boylan and Al Coury
Release date: 17 January 1972
Highest chart place: US: 163
Running time: 31:42

This album lives large in rock 'n' roll mythos because it is here that Linda laid down tracks with her then-current touring band, four of which would go off and form The Eagles. The first time Bernie Leadon, Glenn Frey, Don Henley and Randy Meisner backed Ronstadt was at a concert at, of all places, Disneyland in July 1971.

At that time, Frey was the acknowledged leader of the band and had been selected to be part of Ronstadt's band first. However, J. D. Souther described Henley as the 'Secret Weapon' because he could 'sing anything he wrapped his voice around… that insanely beautiful voice, like four-hundred-grain sandpaper, rough but fine, was incredible to hear, even if you didn't know where it was coming from'.

In his book *To The Limit: The Untold Story of The Eagles*, Marc Eliot describes the backing band's talent when supporting Linda Ronstadt: 'It was a band that showed off the individual talents of each member without burying Ronstadt, or perhaps even more important, one another'.

This album seems to be trying to duplicate the sound of Silk Purse but comes up short in many regards due to its tendency to lean very hard in the direction of traditional country music. There is less country rock, let alone pop, on this album and the overall effect seemed to take Ronstadt backwards rather than propel her career forwards.

The album's producer, John Boylan, spoke about the album's intentions: 'A lot of people in L.A. were trying to figure out the perfect country-rock sound. We knew that if we could get the combination right and the songs right, we could have something big. And we thought we had'. The record-buying public and radio stations did not agree; without a radio hit to propel the album overall, it failed to make an impact despite the large amount of talent assembled to make the record. It couldn't get above number 163 on the *Billboard* album chart and spelled the end of Ronstadt's time with Capitol Records, who didn't know what to do with her after the abysmal reception afforded by this effort.

'Rock Me On The Water' (Browne)

Ronstadt got this song from her friend Jackson Browne and released her version months before his own version hit the airwaves around America. Despite having wonderful source material to work with, Linda's version did not resonate with listeners the way Browne's did, as her song only got to number 85 on the *Billboard* Hot 100. Browne's version fared better, climbing to number 48. For a song that has grown in popularity over the years for Browne, it's surprising how tepid the reception was for either version. This was the second and final single from the album. The fact that there were so few singles from the album is a concerning note about Capitol's confidence in the material provided by Ronstadt.

Eliot writes in his book, 'Anyone hearing it for the first time had to wonder whether to dance or pray. Here was a song that sounded uplifting, affirmative, and spiritual, performed with come-hither sexuality by Ronstadt'. Perhaps the issue with the album, and Boylan's vision for it, is that it tried too hard to do too many things. Even with Eliot's analysis, this song gives the reader whiplash trying to wrap their minds around how they should feel about the song and, perhaps, the album itself.

Ronstadt's vocals on the track are close to folk, with wonderful vocal harmonies behind her. Disappointingly, there is no note on the album about who provided the backing vocals for this particular sound, although they sound suspiciously close to harmonizing later heard on Eagles records. Don Henley and Glenn Frey both play on the track, so it is not outside the realm of possibility that they lent their voices to the track as well. The song, as a whole, is in the vein of Ronstadt's other country singles, so it is curious that this did not chart on that side of things for *Billboard*. There is a live version from 1973 that was recorded in Sausalito that gives a picture of how this was sung live. In a difference from the version on the album, her live vocals are much closer to her style on other country-rock hits, removing the folksy warble in her voice that sounded so unusual on vinyl.

'Crazy Arms' (Mooney/Seals)
A former number-one hit on the country chart a decade and a half prior, this track seems like the type of song Ronstadt would have had in rotation for her live shows during the time. In general, this album seems to be mostly made up of songs with which Linda was comfortable and would have been easy for her and her touring band to lay down in the studio. Ronstadt is almost back to her typical country rock vocal form on this track, although she strays to the previous track's folk-tinged delivery on occasion. Furthermore, her vocals are close in phrasing and elocution to those recorded for 'He Dark The Sun' on *Silk Purse*. The instrumental arrangement on this track doesn't sound as slick as the previous one due to the different backing band here. Overall, it is a good track for where Ronstadt was in her career, but it pales in comparison to similarly positioned songs on the albums to come.

'I Won't Be Hangin' Round' (Kaz)
With a different musical arrangement, this song could pass as a blues song. As it was arranged for this album, however, it is a solid country rock track, highlighted by the steel guitar's influence throughout the entirety of the song. Linda is backed by a remarkable trio of women whose influence on the feel of the song is welcomed. Miss Ona, Dianne Davidson and Merry Clayton combine their voices to underscore Ronstadt's message that she won't be begging for love from anyone, especially the subject of the song's lyrics. Of the three, Clayton is the best known to modern audiences, having been one of the participants in the documentary *20 Feet From Stardom* – her vocals played a crucial role on the Rolling Stones' 'Gimme Shelter'. In a fun bit of trivia, Clayton was the first person to release a version of 'The Shoop Shoop Song (It's In His Kiss)', which Ronstadt would sing on television twice later in the decade.

'I Still Miss Someone' (Cash/Cash Jr.)
As a way to further underscore the country feel of this album, Linda next chose this song made famous by Johnny Cash. Although she could have chosen a better-known song by him, the subject matter was more in her wheelhouse and fit into the type of song listeners expected from her. The song gave her plenty of space to wield her voice for a mournful ballad, dripping with longing in a way that hearkened back to 'Long, Long Time'. However, this song doesn't have the same touch because, rather than being

orchestral, the arrangement went deep into country territory with the use of a fiddle. Much like the previous track, it's interesting to consider how the song could have been more effectively interpreted later in Ronstadt's career. The song is another near-miss that may have benefitted from a more able producer than John Boylan, as he seems to have been leaning more into ease than effort when it came to helping Ronstadt with this album.

'In My Reply' (Taylor)
The first side of the album closed with Linda's version of a song written by James Taylor's brother Livingston. While Ronstadt would be more closely identified with Taylor when both were managed by Peter Asher a few years after this album, Livingston was a singer-songwriter in his own right and, similar to Linda, was just beginning his career. The lyrical structure of the song is typical for a tune from this time, as it tells a narrative story as the song progresses. This is one of the strongest songs on the first side of the record and placing it opposite 'Rock Me On The Water' may have been strategic in order to mask some of the weaker material between the two songs. The track draws its strength from the steel guitar work and Linda's gentle vocals. Unlike some of the previous songs on the album, her voice is given more of an opportunity to shine and she sings with more confidence here.

'I Fall To Pieces' (Cochran/Howard)
This is the first time Linda decided to take on a Patsy Cline song and interpret it for herself; she would later go on to do the same to 'Crazy' on *Hasten Down The Wind* to great acclaim. Opening the second side of the album with a well-known song was a clever way to have listeners flip over the record and keep listening – this rendition does just that. For a live recording, it is impeccable; looking back, it's astounding that the technology existed to make such a clean-sounding recording. The crowd doesn't factor into the track at all until they applaud at the end. A second live version from the Sausalito concert gives the listener a chance to enjoy the combination of Ronstadt and her band creating magic.

Ronstadt's vocals are simply beautiful here. She takes on Cline's legend, already grown long despite her untimely passing less than a decade prior, and builds on the legacy of Patsy's beloved song. She makes her own mark on the track, which is something she continued to do throughout her career. This song was released as the lead single from the album, coming out three months prior to the album's release. The song failed to chart, which is almost as astounding as how good it sounded.

'Ramblin' 'Round' (Belly/Guthrie/Lomax)
This track may be one of the most country-tinged songs on the entire album, which speaks volumes of how hard it leaned into that genre – both the banjo and fiddle play prominent parts. Herb Pedersen and Bernie Leadon,

in addition to playing instruments on the track, provide backing vocals for Ronstadt and their voices blend quite well at the tail end of the song. This folk song was penned by Lead Belly, Woody Guthrie and John A. Lomax, so the pedigree of the track was long and steeped in Americana. Linda's vocals are strong as she relates the narrative and is able to show off the power of her voice in several places.

'Birds' (Young)
The surprising aspect of the second side of this record is the difference between the songs recorded live and those recorded in the studio. The energy on the tracks sung live in front of an audience, such as this one, is so different from the ones that were recorded in the studio, such as the previous track. This Neil Young song may have been attractive to Linda due to its imagery of a bird throwing out its wings, showing its full wingspan and flying away from a place it no longer wanted to be. This is also a chance for the listener to hear another combination of harmonies backing Linda, as Henley and Meisner sing together to provide the backdrop against which Ronstadt sings her lead vocals in front of the crowd. While working out the arrangements for the songs, she had a lot of talent to utilize and would use them in different combinations depending on the needs of the song.

'I Ain't Always Been Faithful' (Andersen)
Don Henley's drumming provides the beat as the subdued mid-tempo country song weaves its way through its run time. Although it may not be the shiniest track on the album, Ronstadt shows off a different style of singing – her ability to communicate compellingly with a quieter vocal style is clear here. The placement of the song on the album is smart, as it serves as a cool-down before another upbeat song. The dichotomy between Ronstadt's two main musical interests at this time, country and rock, is never more apparent than on this album. While some aspect of blending the two genres was still in its infancy, as it would swiftly overtake the California music scene within just a year or two, this album is a prime example of how the growing pains could be evident to not only listeners but also to the record companies.

'Rescue Me' (Miner/Smith)
Ronstadt closed out the album with a raucous version of the song made most famous by Fontella Bass. As her backing vocalists, she had the magical combination of Frey, Meisner and Henley pushing their voices into high falsetto; they also get into the action during a call-and-response section at the end of the song. This is the third and final track from the album that was recorded live and its exciting energy leaves the listener questioning why it wasn't released as a single. Ronstadt growls through vocals on the track and provides her own tambourine work, as she would during her concerts at this time. The fun she and her band had in singing this song is audibly evident, as

the infectious energy practically oozes out of the speakers. The choicc not to include more live tracks on the album is mystifying in retrospect, as they are among the best-sounding and memorable songs on the entire album. It makes the listener want to go back and be in one of those crowds. In contrast, the studio tracks feel a bit stale and are left wanting for the energy poured into a live performance.

Bonus Tracks

'Kate' (Frey)

This track was included on the expanded release of Ronstadt's Capitol recordings in 2006 and is a live recording from the Troubadour, which means it was most likely recorded during the same show as the three live tracks on the album. Certainly, the audio fidelity speaks to that probability, as the sound is very clear and crisp. One of the reasons why this song may have been excluded from the album is Glenn Frey's prominent vocals, as the song can almost be hailed as a duet rather than one solely focused on Linda's vocals.

The track is also rockier than anything on the album. It sounds like an early Eagles song and this album, or The Eagles' first album, may have benefitted from its inclusion. It's a great way to experience a bunch of superstars playing together at the beginning of their careers. Ronstadt lets loose with a good excuse of singing a rock song and you can hear where she would develop her country-rock voice from here moving forward. An outtake such as this really makes the listener wonder why the record company didn't just opt to record a full album of live music like this.

'Can It Be True' (Karlin/Kymry)

This song was the B-side to 'I Fall To Pieces' and, similar to the previous song, was unreleased in any format, except the original 45, until 2006. Unlike the preceding track, this is along the lines of the ballads found elsewhere on the album. Ronstadt's voice drips with emotion as she runs through a plethora of questions aimed at the subject of her affections. It sounds like a few other laments in pop music at the time and is reminiscent, in sentiment and musicality, of artists such as Petula Clark, Carpenters and Nancy Sinatra. It is much more pop than country and, again, if the overall push for the album hadn't been country-rock (which, arguably, it didn't quite achieve), this would have been a fun track to put on the album rather than consign it to the B-side of a single.

Don't Cry Now (1973)

Personnel:
Linda Ronstadt: lead vocals, tambourine, backing vocals
Spooner Oldham: acoustic piano
John Boylan: electric piano
Craig Doerge: acoustic piano
J. D. Souther: acoustic guitar, bass, electric guitar, backing vocals
Jerry McGee: electric guitar
"Sneaky" Pete Kleinow: steel guitar
Richard Bowden: electric guitar
Andy Johnson: electric guitar
Herb Pedersen: acoustic guitar, backing vocals
Ed Black: steel guitar, electric guitar
Larry Carlton: electric guitar
Buddy Emmons: pedal steel guitar
Rick Roberts: acoustic guitar
Glenn Frey: electric guitar, steel guitar
Mike Bowden: bass guitar
Chris Ethridge: bass guitar
Leland Sklar: bass guitar
Dennis St. John: drums
Mickey McGee: drums
Russ Kunkel: drums
Jimmie Fadden: harmonica
Gib Guilbeau: fiddle
Jim Gordon: saxophone
Nino Tempo: saxophone
Gail Martin: trombone
McKinley Johnson: trumpet
Darrell Leonard: trumpet
Jim Ed Norman: horn arrangements, string arrangements
Jimmie Haskell: string arrangements
Sid Sharp: concertmaster
Ginger Holladay: backing vocals
Mary Holliday: backing vocals
Clydie King: backing vocals
Sherlie Matthews: backing vocals
Marti McCall: backing vocals
Wendy Waldman: backing vocals
Produced between 1972 and 1973 by J. D. Souther, John Boylan and Peter Asher
Release date: 1 October 1973
Highest chart place: US: 45
Running time: 35:34

This is an album that, according to a 1975 *Rolling Stone* article, took over a year and $150,000 to produce. The patchwork quality of its tracks, including a huge list of musicians who contributed to it, is the result of it being touched by three different producers, two of which (J. D. Souther and John Boylan) had been in a relationship with Linda Ronstadt either before or during the production of this album. This was the last of her albums to be produced by someone with whom she was in a personal relationship, as the benefit of separating her personal life and professional career became apparent through the creation of this album.

Thus, it was a rocky start to her career with Asylum Records. She began production with John Boylan but realized his production style wasn't getting her what she wanted for the record. As she shared with Ben Fong-Torres of *Rolling Stone* in 1975, the deterioration of their personal relationship had a direct impact on the professional relationship they had in the production of this album. She also communicated Peter Asher's desire to produce the entire album, but she was too hesitant to move into another producer relationship when her experience was quite shaken in trying to get this album off the ground.

Ronstadt ultimately asked Asher to produce two songs that made it onto the album. A third was considered 'terrible' by Asher and the recordings were resigned to the trash heap – an old hit by Betty Everett called 'You're No Good'. As Asher told *Rolling Stone*, 'I had the wrong rhythm section. They were very good, but they were playing the wrong kind of thing. We gave up'.

After the positive production with Asher, Ronstadt returned to the studio to re-record the majority of the tracks with J. D. Souther:

> We were like kids in the studio, just inept, and we took a lot of time. But I learned a lot and it was worth it, almost, because it was such hard work. After that experience, I knew so much more when I went into the studio with Peter, so it was easier for me to talk to him; it wasn't like I was a person who didn't know how to do what she wanted to do.

Due to her taking time to learn the production side of the business with this album, she was able to form a very good working relationship with Asher for future albums.

In an interview conducted shortly after this album was completed for inclusion in the 1974 book *Rock'n'Roll Woman* by Katherine Orloff, Ronstadt reflected on where she was as a creator at this time in her career. 'Sometimes I think my mission is to do country rock. I really want people to know what the roots are in country music. I want white people to realize that their music is soulful, too'. Ronstadt continued, 'Even though I mostly listen to black music, I'm incurably white as a singer. I want people to be conscious of white soul and what it is'. It was with this mindset that she made this album, although the influences of rhythm and blues here aren't really to be seen. While that would come on later albums, she did focus on bringing soul to the selections she made for this album, using her voice to articulate the emotions she thought were lacking in contemporary popular music.

The album art is Ronstadt sitting in front of a floral pattern backdrop. It's a muted, soft image that has a country feel due to Linda's large, lacy cuffs and silver and turquoise jewelry. The inner sleeve has a better-known black and white image, taken by Terry Wright, of Ronstadt dressed casually in a t-shirt with earphones on and singing into a microphone in the recording studio.

While reviewing this album for *Crawdaddy* magazine in June 1974, Peter Knobler observed, 'There is a consistency of vision to her most recent album… which is more rejected than rejecting and accepts disappointment as a norm. Odd for the pretty girl on the block'. The way in which Ronstadt chose to interpret songs, starting on this album, gave her an opportunity to carve out a niche for herself that would persist for the several following albums. Ronstadt relished singing ballads and slow songs, sometimes with sad subject matter, as her mission was to elicit emotion with her interpretation. This was a surprise to reviewers of this album, but quickly became the expectation for her output for the remainder of the decade. In fact, it became surprising when she deviated from this pattern. As she laughingly shared with Knobler, 'I don't really believe in happy songs!' In answer to his question about why she sang, Linda said, 'It relieves the load in some way. When you can communicate it to someone, it then becomes a joyous experience, joy in the meaning of release'.

As we can now analyze Ronstadt's career from a distance, we can see this album as the runway from which her career would take off. While it didn't cause a huge public sensation, the elements were all coming together to contribute to her next album. The album was certified gold and rose as high as number 45 on the *Billboard* album chart.

'I Can Almost See It' (Souther)

This J. D. Souther-penned song follows a very traditional country arrangement. Souther, with whom Linda Ronstadt had a personal relationship prior to this album, also produced this track for the album. Thus, it isn't hard to imagine that he took extra care while producing this song to best showcase not only Linda's considerable vocal talents but also the lyrics he had written for her to interpret. The extent of their relationship is alluded to by the fact that this is the first of three Souther songs on the album.

Ronstadt's vocals tread familiar territory for those who had listened to her prior albums. Indeed, this is a standard track for Linda's fans, as it sounds audibly familiar to other songs on the albums prior to this one, as well as from *Heart Like A Wheel* immediately after.

'Love Has No Pride' (Kaz/Titus)

Sneaky Pete, who took on steel guitar duties for this tune, really sets the country tone for the track. Linda has a strong outing with her vocals as she sings about missing the person she loved who walked out on her. Her vocal accents at the end of each chorus underscore the desperation she has for the lost love she is seeking, casting her net wide as she emphasizes her desire with a strong voice, before quietly resolving the chorus by repeating that 'she'd give anything to see you again'. Ginger and Mary Holliday's backing vocals provide a sweet background to the second half of the song. The listener can feel Linda's heartbreak by the time the track ends. It's a very soulful country rock song that fits with the time it was recorded and is a great example of what Linda was capable of putting out into the popular music scene. This song was the first single, coming out on 15 October 1973, shortly after the album itself was released. The production of this song features a stronger reliance upon the band as a whole in comparison to Bonnie Raitt's rendition, which came out a year previous to this album. This was the highest charting single from the album, reaching 51 on the *Billboard* Hot 100.

Johnny Cash, who really had a thing for recording inside correctional institutions, taped a television special in 1976 at the Tennessee State Prison. For this recording, Linda brought along her then-current band, including Andrew Gold, Kenny Edwards and Dan Dugmore to back her up in a live rendition of this song. The special was broadcast in 1977 and brought this song, released half a decade earlier, to an expanded audience, as Linda was then a bankable star with a string of hit albums to serve as her credentials. What began with the album after this one had catapulted her into the stratosphere and gave her the opportunity to return to a recording that may have been lesser known to her newer fans.

Dressed in a blue gingham baby doll dress, Ronstadt belts this song out with the mastery that comes with constantly touring for the better part of a decade. At the end of this rendition, she hits a high note that tells of a Broadway stint just a few years off. The reason why she chose this song is easy: it was one with which she was familiar and fit in with the country theme of the special; it was also one that remained on her tour set list for years leading up to the special. While some of her more recent hits would have been too pop for Johnny Cash, this one is exactly what was needed for a country special.

'Silver Threads And Golden Needles' (Reynolds/Rhodes)

No, this is not the result of a sloppy copy/paste job from a prior album. Rather, Linda chose to re-record and release this song again, the first time being on her debut album. Where this version differed is Ronstadt's hard leaning into the country rock sound she had developed since 1969. The newer nature of the song also lent itself to success on the charts, so the decision was made to release it as the second single from the album, coming out on 4 February 1974. This is definitely the version of the song best known by fans. Herb Pederson's backing vocals perfectly complement Linda's performance for the entirety of the song. Gib Guilbeau's fiddle work meshes very well with Ed Black's steel guitar on the middle eight, contributing to the country rock jam feeling of the track. Linda took the raw material of the song and reworked it into a fast-paced rocker that was conducive to widespread appeal and made a statement on how she had developed as a performer since her debut album. The single rose to number 67 on the *Billboard* Hot 100, while it did considerably better on the Hot Country Chart by reaching number 20.

Two live versions of this song deserve some attention. The first was from Don Kirshner's *Rock Concert*, which included a set by Ronstadt's former backing band, The Eagles. They brought Linda onstage to play this song in 1974 when it was still fresh in people's minds after being released as a single. The vibe of the performance is light years away from the 1969 recording and is much rockier than even the version included on this album. Ronstadt's growling rock vocals are apparent at times, showing her awareness that this style was bringing her more attention by the day. She belts out the lead vocal, which is complemented wonderfully by those of The Eagles.

As listeners tuned into the Johnny Cash special in 1977, they were treated to a version of the song from behind the bars of the Tennessee State Prison. While it may have been selected for this set due to originally being a country tune, Ronstadt once again shows her familiarity with the lyrics and has fun with her road band to do something different, again, with the arrangement of a song that had been a staple for her for almost a decade at this point.

'Desperado' (Henley/Frey)

Linda chose a song penned by two of her former backup bandmates that made it big for the next song on the album. Ronstadt's interpretation of the song allows her the space to showcase her large voice, especially on the last notes of the song. The song opens up with a simple piano arrangement to accompany her voice. Other instruments, including a string arrangement, are added after about 45 seconds. The sound of the song becomes more fleshed out from that point, becoming very full by the time it closes out. Clydie King, Sherlie Matthews and Marti McCall add backing vocals in the latter half of the song. The track ends with a blend of the instrumentation that had been added throughout the song.

Linda sang this with The Eagles backing her at least once for a televised appearance with them on *Don Kirshner's Rock Concert* in 1974. She kept the same arrangement of her version, being accompanied by only a piano for the beginning of the song. When the song opens up after the first verse, she is backed by the wonderful harmonies that The Eagles were so famous for. The video captures the ascendency of both acts as they launch into superstardom and listeners are treated to a performance that both parties are comfortable with, as they had played together so much in the past.

On the album *Live In Hollywood*, released in 2019 but recorded for a television special in 1980, Ronstadt closes the album with a rendition of this song. The arrangement of this version hews closely to her recorded version from almost a decade prior, with the benefit of more vocal maturity and control over her voice. Where it differs, however, is that Ronstadt stripped away every instrument except for the piano. As a result, listeners are given a frozen moment in time to just sit back and appreciate Ronstadt's voice and how she presented this song to live audiences.

During her tour of Japan in 1984 to promote her work with Nelson Riddle and his orchestra, Linda performed the song as a treat to the audience who had expected a setlist full of American standards. This was at a time when Ronstadt was distancing herself from her previous pop recordings in the midst of trying to focus on a different genre, so it's a rare treat. Ronstadt's voice is at its prime and the experience of hearing the song, as arranged by Nelson Riddle for a full orchestra, exceeds all expectations. The mastery she has over this song makes it easy to understand why she chose to end concerts for years with it, even as she did here.

'Don't Cry Now' (Souther)

This is the second of three J. D. Souther-written songs on the album and is where it gets its name. This slow ballad, which is clearly Ronstadt's wheelhouse at this point in time, begins with a slow piano riff, and the country rock sound that is present throughout the album is gently injected. In this way, it is representative of the feeling of the entire album and is a good choice for a title track. The steel guitar woven throughout is especially effective in complementing the sentiments of loss and pain Linda expresses in the course of the song.

The last verse undergoes a key change and allows Ronstadt to push her vocals to a higher register. Since working with Ronstadt in the 1970s, Souther has been quite plainspoken in how he always believed Ronstadt's interpretations of his words were much better than he could have imagined them sounding. On a track like this, it's easy to see how Ronstadt used his lyrics as a firm foundation to layer in her vocals and the instrumental arrangement to come up with something that is greater than the sum of its parts. Despite this song being the title track of a moderately successful album, it didn't feature in live sets beyond the time this album was released. This became a pattern, as the title tracks for the next few albums were chosen more to represent the mood of the album rather than be a crucial part of the touring set assembled by Ronstadt and her band.

'Sail Away' (Newman)

To open up the second side of the record, Ronstadt chose this recent Randy Newman song. From a contemporary point of view, this is considered one of Newman's best tracks of all time; the fact Linda chose it only a year after he released it, shows her keen sense of quality and the desire to work with the best possible material. In a 1972 analysis of the song, *Rolling Stone* writer

Stephen Holden describes the song as presenting an idealized version of America to Africans during the pre-Civil War era. Put against the backdrop of the ongoing Civil Rights struggle in America, Newman's cynical lyrics about how vulnerable populations in America could be taken advantage of by the majority were expertly interpreted by Ronstadt. The message conveyed by this song is still pertinent to American society in the 21st century, as racial disparities have not been resolved and are being exploited by the same type of person who narrates this song.

Musically, this is a soft way to open up the second side of a record. Ronstadt's vocals are strong but subdued, while the backing vocals are reminiscent of a church choir. The musical interpretation of the song belies its more serious message and the listener is caught off-guard by the darker meaning of the lyrics set against such a sunny, warm arrangement. It's a masterful production job and shouldn't be skipped.

'Colorado' (Roberts)

One of the most country-esque songs on the album, the mournful lyrics are powerful tools in Linda's hands as she tells the tale of a woman who just wants her man and her home back in Colorado. The steel guitar wails in agony as she lays her burden down on the listener. The descending chord structure runs parallel to the lyrics, communicating a downward spiral, while the slow tempo and emotive guitar serve to emphasize the inner turmoil caused by her unfulfilled desire. This style of song is what she predominantly became known for in the 1970s and selecting similar material for the following few albums was something the public expected, resulting in her jarring changes of genre as the decade progressed.

This song stayed on her touring set list for at least a few years after this album was released. It was one of the staples people knew her by and she was able to show off her acoustic guitar skills as part of her show due to this song. The sad ballad gave her a chance to slow down a live show and showcase her soaring vocals; even in the midst of a show packed with songs that leaned more heavily into the rock and pop genre, it gave Linda a country song to play with on a consistent basis. It was also one of the increasingly rare opportunities she had, heading into the mid-1970s, to sing without backup during a concert. While many tracks on subsequent albums featured backing from the likes of Andrew Gold or Kenny Edwards, this song remained one she sang with no other vocal support.

'The Fast One' (Souther)

The third and final selection from J. D. Souther here, this song is more of a rocker than either of the prior songs on the second side of the album. Souther played the acoustic guitar on the track, while also complementing Ronstadt's lead vocals with his own harmonizing. This gives us a preview of what their harmonies would achieve a few years later on *Prisoner In*

Disguise, which also featured songs written by Souther. Glenn Frey of The Eagles contributes electric guitar to the track, which is one of the main reasons why it seemed more rock than country, despite the steel guitar also playing a part. In an odd way, Ed Black's steel guitar work contributes to the rock feel of the song, despite the instrument's heavy association with country music.

Souther wasn't unfamiliar with singing this song, as he released it the previous year on his own album. That version featured a more traditional country arrangement. While producing the song for Ronstadt, he would have been open to what she wanted to do with the material. At some point, they decided to call in their friend Glenn to spice up the sound, much to the benefit of the listener.

'Everybody Loves A Winner' (Williams/Jones/Bell)

The album then shifts to a slower tempo with this song, which also has a decidedly more country flavor compared to the prior track. Herb Pederson provides Linda with backing vocals on the chorus as she works her way through a melancholy song about how everyone wants to be in the company of a winner, but when you lose, a person always does that alone. What sets this song apart from the rest of the album is the heavy reliance on a horn section to create a wall of sound behind Ronstadt's vocals. The rich sound this produces may remind listeners of other acts singing the same type of content – for example, Elvis Presley utilized a horn section to great effect in his performances at this time.

With its position on the album – second to last – this song wasn't created to be a hit single. Rather, it was a place to experiment and do something different and unexpected. In this case, it was with the arrangement of the song and its instruments that gave Linda a break from what had been produced so far on the album. There were horns on 'Desperado', but they were blended into the track in a much different way. Not only are the horns much more prominent on this track, but they sound closer to contemporary Elvis Presley arrangements than those featured on the prior track.

'I Believe In You' (Young)

For the closing track on the album, Linda chose a song written by Neil Young. Peter Asher's touch as producer can be felt on this track, as it is constructed much like a traditional rock song. Ronstadt and Asher had a collaborative relationship throughout their time working together and he was able to make her ideas become reality with his handling of the musicians involved. While it is still very much a country rock track, it gives a glimpse into what was immediately ahead for Ronstadt's career.

By having an Asher-produced song in the last position on the album, Linda ensured that those listening to the end would be in for a treat. The backing vocals lend a richness to the production that accentuates Ronstadt's soaring vocals. These are the same back-up vocalists from the beginning of this side of the album; 'Sail Away' was also produced by Asher. It should come as no surprise that two of the tracks with the deftest and most sensitive production on the album were those headed by Asher. It's also significant that the tracks he produced sound like future Ronstadt, whereas the tracks that seemed more run-of-the-mill were produced by Souther or Boylan.

Heart Like A Wheel (1974)

Personnel:
Linda Ronstadt: lead vocals, backing vocals
Andrew Gold: electric piano, electric guitar solo, drums, percussion, acoustic piano, electric rhythm guitar, tambourine, backing vocals, acoustic guitar, ukulele
Eddie Black: electric guitar
Bob Warford: acoustic guitar, electric guitar
"Sneaky" Pete Kleinow: pedal steel guitar
Herb Pedersen: banjo, backing vocals
Paul Craft: acoustic guitar
John Starling: acoustic guitar
Danny Pendleton: pedal steel guitar
John Boylan: acoustic guitar
Glenn Frey: acoustic guitar
Kenny Edwards: bass guitar, backing vocals
Chris Ethridge: bass guitar
Emory Gordy Jr.: bass guitar
Tom Guidera: bass guitar
Timothy B. Schmit: bass guitar
Dennis St. John: drums
Russ Kunkel: drums
Lloyd Myers: drums
Don Henley: drums
Peter Asher: percussion, cowbell, backing vocals
Jimmie Fadden: harmonica
David Lindley: fiddle
Gregory Rose: string arrangements and conductor
David Campbell: string arrangements, viola
Dennis Karmazyn: cello
Richard Feves: double bass
Clydie King: backing vocals
Sherlie Matthews: backing vocals
Wendy Waldman: backing vocals
Cissy Houston: backing vocals
Joyce Nesbitt: backing vocals
Maria Muldaur: backing vocals
Emmylou Harris: harmony vocals
Produced at The Sound Factory and Clover Recorders, Los Angeles; Track Recorders, Maryland; Record Plant and The Hit Factory, New York City; Trident Studios and AIR Studios, London, between June and September 1974 by Peter Asher
Release date: 19 November 1974
Highest chart places: US: 1
Running time: 31:40

After her first successful Asylum release with *Don't Cry Now*, Linda Ronstadt needed to complete her contractual obligation to Capitol Records and give them one more album. The canny Ronstadt not only produced a historic album (and knew it) but played the two record companies against one another when it came to promoting the album. Capitol wanted to show Asylum it could beat the newer company when it came to record promotion, so poured tons of resources into the campaign. At the same time, Asylum boss David Geffen knew that moving forward, Ronstadt would be their artist – so, as Linda wrote in her memoir, '[the next record] would sell more [for Asylum] if the Capitol record sold well'. When Linda set out to make this record in 1974, she had a simple goal: all she wanted to do was make enough money to buy a washing machine. 'Lugging heavy bags full of dirty clothes to the Fluff 'n' Fold on the two days I had off before starting another tour was a drag'.

Capitol, for its part, wanted to go out with a bang with this record. Even though, as Linda wrote, they wanted her to either pick country or rock to sing (she refused), she finally convinced them to let her sign with another company because they already had Helen Reddy (whose records were regularly sold out due to her popularity) and Anne Murray. They didn't know what to do with her, so Capitol thought she was Asylum's creative conundrum after this record was out.

This album was Linda Ronstadt's breakthrough and charted not only in the top spot of the *Billboard* country album charts but also the Top 200 album chart. 'When 'Heart Like A Wheel' went to Number One', Linda told *Rolling Stone*'s Cameron Crowe in 1976:

> I just walked around apologizing every single day. I could see that my supposed friends resented me. I went around going, 'I'm not that good of a singer…' And I got so self-conscious that when I went onstage, I couldn't sing at all. It almost made me go crazy… I mean I needed a lot of help, you know.

This was also her first album to go platinum (it has actually gone double platinum), was selected for preservation by the Library of Congress due to its cultural importance and has been lauded as a masterpiece since its release. The album was nominated for several Grammys, including for Peter Asher's work as producer, Album Of The Year and Best Pop Vocal Performance, Female. Although it only scored one Grammy, the importance of the album in Ronstadt's career far outweighed any award.

Needless to say, Ronstadt was able to buy a washing machine after this album.

'You're No Good' (Ballard Jr.)

The first successful version of this song was recorded and released in 1963 by Betty Everett. However, by the standard Linda would later set with the song, it wasn't overly successful, rising only to number 51 on the *Billboard* charts that year.

As Linda embarked on her first full album with producer Peter Asher, along with Andrew Gold as a member of her band, she was looking to switch up the formula for her sound. While her past albums had been mostly country rock, they had limited chart success, and her biggest hit to date 'Long, Long Time' was more in the pattern of 'Different Drum' from her time with The Stone Poneys than something that sounded like a hit rock or pop record. Kenny Edwards suggested this song and she had been trying it out in her live performances since 1973. 'We would be jamming during rehearsal and Kenny said, "Why don't we do this, it would be fun?"' Ronstadt told *Mix Online*. 'I'm a ballad singer and in a lot of the venues we were playing, the air conditioning was louder than we were. So we had to have a couple of up-tempo songs to open and close with. And that was a really good closer'.

As Ben Fong-Torres wrote in a 1975 article for *Rolling Stone*, 'One of her better songs on the *Young* tour was a version of the old Betty Everett hit 'You're No Good..." As written about earlier, Linda tried recording this song for her last album, but it wasn't to be. In an odd coincidence, considering the later success of this song, Ronstadt sang it immediately after 'Long, Long Time' in a December 1973 episode of *The Midnight Special*. This song marks a clear delineation between her career before and after widespread mainstream success.

This time, with the past failure of recording this song on her mind, Ronstadt was determined to try it again. The addition of Gold to the musical mix was the necessary spark for this and other songs to succeed; Gold's talents as a multi-instrumentalist, as well as his lineage coming from a very musical family very different from Ronstadt's own musical family history, were catalysts in creating a different sort of sound in the studio. Gold could create a rockier sound unheard of on previous Ronstadt albums. Fong-Torres wrote that while song choices were Linda's, musical arrangements were a collaboration between her, Asher and Gold. In a 1976 article for *Rolling Stone*, Cameron Crowe described the song as 'a mainstream pop effort stronger and more confident than anything she'd ever recorded'. The decision to return to this song came about a month into sessions for the album. The prior arrangement, which was closer to R&B, was tossed out, the new one was crafted and the rest is musical history. 'We were tired of the arrangement we had been playing on stage and decided to try something new', wrote Ronstadt in her memoir.

Gold starts the track off with a swampy-sounding guitar, before being joined by a matching guitar. Of note, Gold has a soaring, phenomenal guitar solo in the middle of the song, which gives Linda a springboard to launch a very raw-sounding final chorus.

'The first time I heard it on the radio, I said, "That sucker's a hit". I just knew it', Ronstadt told *Mix Online*. 'It's really a well-constructed record. I have to give Peter and Andrew credit'. The sucker was, indeed, a hit, going all the way to number one on the *Billboard* chart and giving Linda her first smash success. Even if she wasn't particularly fond of the song later in her career, telling the *Deseret News* in 1993 that 'I thought the production on 'You're No Good' was very good, but I didn't sing it very well. As a song, it was just an afterthought. It's not the kind of song I got a lot of satisfaction out of singing'. This is in line with most of Ronstadt's thoughts on her past work and shows that she is her own harshest critic.

'It Doesn't Matter Anymore' (Anka)

Covering a Buddy Holly classic can be a formidable task for any artist, especially in the 1970s when his legend was only growing due to his influence on seemingly everyone in the industry. However, this type of song was perfectly suited for the material Ronstadt would choose moving forward. Taking a well-worn classic, in this case written by Paul Anka specifically for Buddy Holly, and shaping it into an arrangement for her voice and talents is something she would rely upon for the remainder of her pop music career and this, in combination with Asher's prowess at finding the right musicians, created magic on vinyl.

This was the exact type of crossover hit that established Linda on more than one music chart. This song, for example, charted on three different *Billboard* charts at the same time: Adult Contemporary, Country and Hot 100. It was most popular on the Adult Contemporary chart due to its softer sound but still rose to number 47 on the Hot 100. This is all rather impressive when considering this was the last single from the album, coming out more than four months after the album's release – and six months to the day prior to the release of her next album. The combined efforts of Bob Warford and Sneaky Pete Kleinow on acoustic and steel pedal guitar, respectively, are a nod to its country rock roots and Ronstadt's own background in that musical style. Linda had worked out the guitar arrangement while waxing the floors in her apartment, as she shared in her memoir. Wendy Waldman's voice melds beautifully with Linda's on the vocal tracks and the mournful lament of this song is felt bone-deep by the listener.

'Faithless Love' (Souther)

Guest musician – J. D. Souther: acoustic guitar, harmony vocals

Herb Pedersen's banjo picking opens this track in a perfect way to frame it, initially, as a country song. Even the title of the song evokes a country music feel. The other star backing player on this song is the writer of the song himself, J. D. Souther, who takes on harmony vocals and acoustic guitar duties and joins Ronstadt in crafting a beautiful interpretation that would feature in Linda's set lists for years to come. Linda wouldn't keep a song around for a long time unless she truly enjoyed singing it, as touring meant singing the same songs over and over again. At a 1977 concert, she introduced the song as being by J. D. Souther, 'my favorite California songwriter and one of my favorite singers'. Linda reflected in her memoir that Souther wrote this song while they were still in a relationship together, 'hole[d] up with our books and our music'. Andrew Gold's touch on the acoustic and electric pianos lifts this song from a country tune to a pop music ballad. While the banjo is present throughout, it doesn't necessarily constrain the track to being pure country. But why did she choose this, among other similar songs? 'I've been heartbroken a lot. That's a keyword', she told *Rolling Stone*'s Ben Fong-Torres.

This song is a brilliant example of how Ronstadt could take a song and have it develop beyond what she initially put down on vinyl. It's the type of song she would revisit over and over on tours and find something new to develop and grow, despite having sung it many times before. Even here, on this record, there is more than enough harmony and musicality to make it a classic. Putting this track immediately after 'It Doesn't Matter Anymore' makes them a formidable pair when listened to back-to-back as they strike a similar tone.

'The Dark End Of The Street' (Moman/Penn)
This is another song that was piloted by Ronstadt while touring before it made its appearance on vinyl as an album track. A recording of this song's pre-album version is available because it was broadcast by a Los Angeles radio station live from the Record Plant studios in the fall of 1973. The original version of the song is stripped down and features no backing vocals and a tad more country flavor.

By the time Linda and company recorded it the following year, the arrangement had been beefed up a bit through the magical trio of herself, Asher and Gold. The backing vocals laid down by Ronstadt over multiple layered tracks were added to by Cissy Houston (mother of Whitney) and Joyce Nesbitt to make a wall of audio that injects soul into this simple country track. Andrew Gold's touches with the electric rhythm guitar also stand out as something that elevates the song to a more intricate yet intimate level. While the song could never serve as a single, as it wouldn't have the ability to chart on its own, it does its job well on the first side of the album and fits the mood made apparent by this point on the record. It's torchy in all the right ways and sets the scene for the next song, which would close out the first side of the record.

'Heart Like A Wheel' (McGarrigle)
'I felt like a bomb had exploded in my mind', wrote Ronstadt about hearing this song for the first time, 'The song, both plainspoken and delicate, had a highly original approach to describing the peril of romantic love'. After receiving the recording by McGarrigle sisters Anne (who also wrote the song) and Kate, Ronstadt asserted that 'it rearranged my entire musical landscape'. Choosing a song by the duo to interpret was an unusual choice, as even Linda admits that they 'defied categorization and were not understood by all'.

'Kate and Anna opened a door for me and I scooted through it as fast as I could', reflected Ronstadt. Part of that scooting involved taking the raw material that the McGarrigle sisters laid down on tape and interpreting it for her singular voice and the sound she was developing for this album. Ronstadt originally didn't consult Asher about its inclusion, as she 'couldn't bear to see the song rejected'. She tacked it onto a show at Carnegie Hall and played it live after a bit of a musical nudge by Gold in rehearsal. Thus, in early 1974, the development of this song as one of her own began. 'The lyric just said everything I felt', Ronstadt shared in a 2023 interview with Jeff Kahliss of the Alta Journal, 'about something that you're stuck in but you're going to get out of'.

The construction of the song included the vocals reinterpreted for a solo singer, but Ronstadt also tapped into the talents of David Campbell to arrange the strings for the entire song. Campbell wrote everything for the strings, including a cello solo that Linda was adamant about including. Without the string arrangement, Ronstadt wouldn't have been able to communicate the strength of her emotions as effectively. Maria Muldaur, one of Linda's friends, took a break from the oasis to contribute backing vocals. It's an unforgettable song to end side one of the record and can be seen as the album's summary statement. In short, it is perfectly slotted, sung and played.

'When Will I Be Loved' (Everly)

The sound evoked by this song is what fans would come to expect from this new era of Ronstadt's career: strong singing, a rocking backup band and material reimagined for the new decade. This song, along with 'It Doesn't Matter Anymore', was released as a single on 25 March 1975. Although there were four singles from the album, they were all released as a duo so that stations had a chance to choose which record to spin based on their demographic. Each release had a more country-leaning song, as well as one more oriented for rock and pop radio. This song was the rock single, so it was the one more heavily promoted on popular music stations around the United States. The single was a slow burn on the charts, eventually peaking at the number two spot for two weeks in June of 1975 (by which time Ronstadt was completing her next album). Despite being more rock-oriented than its reverse side single, this song reached number one on the *Billboard* Country & Western chart, which showed Ronstadt's continued appeal to those listeners. According to a *New York Times* article published at the time of the album's release, the record company vacillated between releasing this song or 'You're No Good' as the lead single, eventually settling upon the latter.

Much like the previous song on the album, Linda arranged the song for a singular, rather than duo, lead vocal. The original version of the song by the Everly Brothers was decidedly old-fashioned by the time Ronstadt recorded her version – the musical landscape had changed significantly since 1960. Ronstadt flipped the first and fourth verses around and had Kenny Edwards and Andrew Gold sing alongside her for the choruses. It's an excellent, upbeat song to start the second side of the record that still maintains the basic theme of the album as a whole.

'Willin'' (George)
This song began a string of three on this side of the album that were more country than most of the tracks on the first side. Ronstadt's fans from her days recording more country-oriented songs could rejoice in this return to that sound, although it had been vastly updated in both arrangement and content compared to her previous efforts in the field. This is the first song Linda chose from Lowell George and his band Little Feat and is her best effort at gelling her sound with his words. While low-key enough for the country crowds, it was also loud enough for her to play regularly in concert for years to come and is also an excellent example of a track that gave her room to break out her rock 'n' roll voice and let it blast.

This song remained a staple in Ronstadt concerts and was a constant on her setlist up until the time she stopped playing pop music in concert in 1982, at which point she switched to touring American standards. The version from a 1982 Dallas-area radio broadcast showcased her voice after she had done extensive vocal training for Broadway and if 1974 audiences were blown away by her vocals, then, they were in for a treat once they tuned in to hear this one. The most easily accessible version of a live performance of this song appears on Ronstadt's 1980 *Live In Hollywood* album, produced for an HBO special of the same name. This special showcased Ronstadt's ability to effortlessly deliver songs from her back catalog and this track, especially, gave her the ability to highlight her vocal prowess.

'I Can't Help It (If I'm Still In Love With You)' (Williams)
Ronstadt returns to a Hank Williams classic for her next song. The track is easily the most traditional country song on the album. Ronstadt's friend Emmylou Harris flew out to help her with the task of vocal duties, with whom she had worked out harmonies prior to recording. Listeners were in for a treat when these two women combined forces to create the most beautiful harmonies. This song was released alongside 'You're No Good' on the flip side, thereby providing country music stations with a single to promote the same day the album dropped. The song was very successful on the *Billboard* Hot Country Singles chart, where it reached number two. It also won Ronstadt her first Grammy award for Best Country Vocal Performance, Female at the 1976 awards show. Seeing Ronstadt sing this song live in 1975, Ben Fong-Torres wrote, 'Linda is able to express multiple emotions in a single phrase, snarling out one word and crying another in 'I Can't Help It if I'm Still in Love with You'. Hot-pointed anger and heartbroken concession all at once'.

Emmylou and Linda performed this song for Dolly Parton's televised variety show in the late 1970s, with Ronstadt playing the acoustic guitar on stage as well as handling vocals. Ronstadt performed this for her own televised special in 1980, but it did not make the cut for official release on her *Live In Hollywood* album release in 2019. The exclusion from the album is a bit curious; while other unreleased tracks from this special may have been held back because they were particular to the album being released at that time (*Mad Love*), and didn't fit the mold of a 2019 album release that would need her bigger hits represented, it's hard to argue that this wasn't a big enough hit. That means that, most likely, it did not meet the quality standard for Ronstadt to okay its inclusion or, perhaps just as likely, it didn't fit on the album (although, in the current day, space considerations for an album aren't what they used to be).

'Keep Me From Blowing Away' (Craft)
The inclusion of this song was serendipitous and the result of a bad case of the flu Linda came down with while touring in 1974. As she writes in her memoir, she needed to take some time off after performing a date in Washington D.C. While staying at friend John Starling's house in Maryland, she recuperated over a number of days and emerged to find the writer of this song, Paul Craft, playing it. Ronstadt was so enthusiastic that she asked Craft and Starling to record it with her then and there on the East Coast. They utilized the recording studio of George Massenberg, who would go on to play a large part in Linda's professional life. 'He would eventually become my most important musical partner, working together [with me] on at least 16 albums', Ronstadt wrote in her memoir.

The song fits in with Ronstadt's style of singing a torchy ballad and the guitar work on the track is resplendent in its ability to almost sing alongside her. This song may be the most overlooked on the album due to its lesser-known writer and musical contributors, which is a disservice to a track that, if given a chance, will stay with the listener for quite some time after it ends. Ronstadt was the guest of The Seldom Scene for a 1986 concert and sang this while backed by them. It is a singularly gorgeous rendition that uses Linda's expanded vocal maturity and training to its benefit.

'You Can Close Your Eyes' (Taylor)
This track presents a sort of Eagles meeting point, with current (Glenn Frey, Don Henley) and future (Timothy B. Schmit) members lending their talents to back up Ronstadt's delicate rendition of a James Taylor song. Linda's producer, Peter Asher lends backing vocals and her past producer John Boylan plays guitar. It's an explosive amount of talent for a track that wasn't a single, but easily could have been.

The choice of this song to end the album is appropriate, as the lyrics provide a sense of closure; although the sun is literally going down in the song, Ronstadt also gives hope that another day is right around the corner. Moreover, this can be understood in terms of Linda's career; even though this album was closing out, it would more than likely be followed by another album relatively quickly.

Bonus Track

'Drift Away/Rip It Up Medley' (Williams) (Blackwell/Marascalco)
Linda made an appearance on Cher's variety show and performed this wonderful medley with the host. More than any other television performance, Ronstadt is taken out of her typical element. Dressed in a sparkly, flowing dress (perhaps by Bob Mackie) and with a wig larger than most, sported by her friend Dolly Parton, Linda and Cher dig into two rock songs: one from the recent past and one from the annals of rock history. Ronstadt indulges in the performance, communicated by her intense body language, as the two icons sing the slower 'Drift Away' before kicking into a higher gear with 'Rip It Up'. There were only so many songs Linda could fit onto an album and, sadly, neither of these were ever recorded for a standard release, although Ronstadt sings them both with affection and familiarity. This television appearance was mere days before the second set of singles was released from the album, so appearing with Cher was a promotional move to keep the momentum going.

Prisoner In Disguise (1975)

Personnel:
Linda Ronstadt: lead vocals
Andrew Gold: acoustic guitar, handclaps, backing vocals, acoustic piano, synthesizers, tambourine, electric piano, electric guitar, drums, congas, Hammond organ, bagpipes
Herb Pedersen: banjo, backing vocals
Dan Dugmore: steel guitar
Lowell George: slide guitar
Danny Kortchmar: electric guitar
J. D. Souther: acoustic guitar, harmony vocals
David Grisman: mandolin
James Taylor: acoustic guitar
Ed Black: electric guitar
Glen Hardin: acoustic piano
Kenny Edwards: bass guitar, backing vocals
Russ Kunkel: drums
Nigel Olsson: drums
David Kemper: drums
Peter Asher: shaker, tambourine, handclaps, guitar, cowbell, cabasa, backing vocals, bagpipes
Jim Conner: harmonica
David Lindley: fiddle
David Campbell: string arrangements and conductor
Don Francisco: backing vocals
Maria Muldaur: harmony vocals
Pat Henderson: backing vocals
Julia Tillman Waters: backing vocals
Maxine Willard Waters: backing vocals
Produced at Sound Factory between February and June 1975 by Peter Asher
Release date: 15 September 1975
Highest chart place: US: 4
Running time: 35:57

Linda Ronstadt and her team faced the enviable task of following up a smash record beloved by critics and fans. Now that she had burst onto a scene that she had been a part of for years, she was faced with carefully choosing a selection of songs that would make a mark and continue her success. Linda would turn to songs written by others instead of any written by herself, explaining to *People* magazine, in a piece published in November 1975, that 'I'd hate to add to the ever-increasing pile of bad songs'. Like its predecessor, this album would quickly go platinum – a feat that, at that time, hadn't been accomplished by any other female artist. Although she had future plans on where to go musically, she stayed close to the formula that had made her successful so far. In an October 1975 article, Linda was quoted as saying, 'I don't just want to retread old songs, but I will continue to go backwards to go forwards'. In essence, even in 1975, she was playing the popular music game, appealing to the widest possible fan base in order to secure more musical freedom later on in her career. Ronstadt's forward-thinking nature and career planning were present even as this album was released, as there's a mention in *Newsweek* of her wanting to record a Mexican album a dozen years before such an album was created and released.

Mixing styles also seemed to work for Ronstadt on her previous album, so she continued to select songs from across genres. Reviewing *Prisoner In Disguise, Parade* magazine said: 'a superb collection of twangy, bittersweet ballads, the album has sufficiently broad appeal to attract both country and rock audiences'. Linda knew her bread was buttered on both sides; on one side, she had her rock and pop fans, while country lovers were the other half. In order to make this record a hit, she knew she needed widespread appeal that would hit multiple charts at the same time.

Some tracks were pulled together in a matter of an hour, while others were arduously crafted over the course of many days. This album was released less than a year after *Heart Like A Wheel* and had to capitalize on that album becoming insanely popular at the beginning of the calendar year – so time was of the essence.

Linda's blend of songs met success when it came to the record-buying public, who also pushed her songs up the charts on popular radio, but critics weren't won over so quickly by this album's effort. One of those critics was Margo Jefferson in *Newsweek*, who said, '*Prisoner In Disguise* shows the success – and occasional failure – of Ronstadt's struggle to balance tradition, eclecticism and originality. Two Motown songs miss because she fails to catch soul music's sly, sassy phrasing'. Critics would continue in this vein for the remainder of Ronstadt's career, despite her success on the charts, at the concert box office and in sales.

The album art, much like that of the record before it, was sparse. It showed Ronstadt as a prisoner inside the design of the jacket – a plaintive figure sitting in a blue box, with a large black area surrounding the whole. Kosh, who would go on to design many of Ronstadt's album covers, recalled his desire to work with Ronstadt on this album because 'her artistry rose above all others'. The photograph of Ronstadt was taken by Ethan Russell, a noted rock 'n' roll photographer. The inside gatefold of the album was given over to lyrics for all of the songs contained within the album. This isn't dissimilar from what one would find on other albums; what sets it apart is the handwritten lyrics, mostly by those songwriters themselves. Ronstadt wasn't hiding that she interpreted the words of others when she made an album. Rather, she gave them even more credit by asking them to provide handwritten lyrics for everyone to see. You also get a sense of who these songwriters are – all of them recording artists in their own right. From Dolly

Parton's wonderful cursive to James Taylor's blocky printing, listeners were able to connect with the songs visually as well as audibly.

'Love Is A Rose' (Young)

This first track was written by Neil Young for an album he recorded in 1974 entitled *Homegrown*. That album wasn't released and Linda was able to record her own version, which came out a full two years before Young released his own. Peter Asher, Ronstadt's producer, is the one who approached Young for the song, as noted in a *Rolling Stone* article on the album. When Young's version was finally released, it was on a compilation record, meaning Ronstadt's version is the one that received the most exposure, especially considering the platinum status *Prisoner In Disguise* quickly achieved. This song was also the lead single from the album, released on 18 August 1975. As summer turned to fall, it rose to number 65 on the *Billboard* Hot 100 charts. As is typical for many Ronstadt releases of this era, it also charted on the *Billboard* Hot Country Singles chart, reaching number five on 29 November 1975.

Herb Pedersen's banjo work opens the track, paving the way for Ronstadt to lay down her vocals. The song is evocative of a hoedown, which is one of the locations specifically sung about by Linda here. The upbeat tempo is something noted in an article about the song on Rhino Record's website; it is a marked contrast from Neil Young's original recording of the song, which featured a prominent harmonica part that made the original very folksy in comparison to Ronstadt's take.

The choice of this track as the lead single made a lot of sense from a business standpoint. Ronstadt, known mostly for her slower songs, needed an energetic track to grab the public's attention and show that this album would be as rocking as *Heart Like A Wheel*. The song is a fun romp through the country with Linda and company, as it treads the familiar territory of country rock and a wonderfully produced backing band that listeners had become familiar with the previous year. The lead single also bore the responsibility for setting the expectation for the upcoming album, as this was released a month prior to the full album release. This was Linda's chance to grab the listener's attention.

As sales pitches go, this one makes its case in two minutes and 16 seconds. The faster tempo makes this song pass by almost too quickly while giving you a taste of the strong vocals Ronstadt brings to the table. Andrew Gold continued to contribute his backing vocals and instrumental mastery on this album and they are both on display here. Furthermore, Kenny Edwards excels in supporting his Stone Poneys frontwoman here and throughout the album. In a December 1975 article, *Rolling Stone* noted that the recording of this song went quickly; it sounds like a fun jam session that just happened to turn into an album track. In the same article, Gold described this song as having a 'funky barn dance' feel. Most of the elements of this song were recorded in about an hour, according to Gold, with everything sort of just gelling together to create a quick, painless recording session.

'Hey Mister, That's Me Up On The Jukebox' (Taylor)
James Taylor, also managed by Peter Asher, originally released his version of this song in 1971 on his *Mud Slide Slim And The Blue Horizon* album. Ronstadt's working relationship with the songwriter, then, would have been somewhat friendlier since she was familiar with Taylor and would have been accustomed to his ways of creating. Ronstadt had the benefit of having drummer Russ Kunkel, who also played for Taylor, play on her version. Kunkel's drumming is a bit more subtle here, as Ronstadt's version verges on ballad rather than rock.

Dan Dugmore's steel guitar is prominent and provides an emotional counterpoint to the piano on the track; while the piano playing is pretty straightforward, Dugmore makes the steel guitar weep alongside Linda's voice. When Ronstadt adds her vocals in combination with the steel guitar, the effect is almost haunting and you understand how desperate the narrator is to move beyond their song that's contained within that jukebox. This track is also the first to feature David Campbell's string arrangements; whether subtle or obvious, strings are strongly present on the album's first side.

The lyric 'I've been spreading myself thin these days' resonates with a lot of listeners, as they multitask work and home life in the midst of world events that can sometimes add stress to the already full routine. In short, it gives listeners a connection point they can attach and hold onto. Andrew Gold's simple piano work throughout makes the track seem appropriately lonely and gives Dugmore something to weave around. The listener is left desolate once Ronstadt closes out her vocal, allowing only a moment to take a deep breath.

'Roll Um Easy' (George)
Ronstadt had found success with Lowell George's 'Willin'' on her previous album, so she went back to his work for a track here as well. She chose one that comes off a bit harder than 'Willin'', with a strong drum beat to guide the listener along. Ronstadt was close with George and in her memoirs, she says her favorite rock band of all time was his band, Little Feat. Thus, it is no surprise that she was able to land George's slide guitar playing on this track; after all, he knew the song better than anyone, having written and performed it himself.

Ronstadt's version took a song that was originally very sparse and transformed it into a country rock song that managed to fit the feel of the album she was recording at the time. Her vocals are strong and punctuate the lyrics that were originally smooth and syrupy. You can see Ronstadt striving to have an edge with the recording of this track, setting herself apart from her balladic material.

Ronstadt benefitted from recording the song in such a manner. As she writes in her memoir, not every song could be a ballad, especially when considering the setlist for a tour. The advantage of recording a rocker like this meant that she could insert this into future concert tours to break up the soaring ballads for which she was best known and, perhaps, what she favored when constructing an album. Additionally, harder songs could survive the acoustics of stadiums that Linda was starting to play; drums and heavy guitar parts could survive these large spaces, whereas softer songs were harder to get right in terms of sound. It also gave her a chance to showcase harder vocals that allowed her to break out from those she typically displayed in her sadder songs. 'Roll Um Easy' had a shorter shelf life than 'Willin'', however, and is probably only familiar to those who listen to albums as a whole. While 'Willin'' featured in concerts for years to come, 'Roll Um Easy' disappeared into Ronstadt's back catalog quite quickly.

'Tracks Of My Tears' (Moore/Robinson/Tarplin)

This was the third and final single released from the album, coming out on 8 December 1975 – almost three months after the album was released. This was most likely done to help boost sales of the album during the holiday season, as those who may have missed out when it was first released may have wanted it to be underneath the Christmas tree. Relying upon a song originally done by Smokey Robinson and the Miracles was a savvy move by Asylum Records, as they relied on song recognition to generate a last push of sales – not that the album needed it by that time, as it was already a huge hit.

This was Ronstadt's first time covering Smokey Robinson, an artist she held in high esteem. Reworking the Motown classic in her own way, there was more than a hint of country-inspired steel guitar work by Dan Dugmore to set the tone. Ronstadt effectively interprets the lyrics and combines very strong vocals with those of Andrew Gold, Kenny Edwards, Peter Asher and Herb Pedersen as her backing vocalists. The backing vocals provide a backdrop against which Ronstadt is able to showcase her emotionally resonant lead and allow her the opportunity to hit some very high notes. This may be one of the first times Linda attempts to record consistently high notes on one track and when compared to her later work after vocal training, you can tell that the raw material shown here would be developed into a more confident vocal style capable of hitting these high notes comfortably.

Critical reception of this song was divided, with a 1975 article in *Newsweek* saying that her cover of the Miracles' track missed the mark and a 1977 *Time* magazine article saying that she improved upon the original. The 1977 analysis may be colored by the fact that Ronstadt had two more hit albums to her credit by the time it was written, while the 1975 article may be colored by critics not being used to Ronstadt's wild interpretations.

As part of the effort to promote the song, the record company recorded a proto-music video. In it, we see Peter Asher in the control booth before coverage cuts to the recording studio, where Ronstadt (sporting a red peasant blouse) sings in front of a microphone while backed by her band. The real magic of this video is seeing how Ronstadt sang in the recording studio. Ronstadt faces her band while recording so that there is full communication between singer and band. The video ends with the outro we're used to from the album track and Ronstadt giving a small smile. However, the most special part of this video is that it is an alternate take of the recording. This video was done live, meaning everything was done in the studio together at the same time. Rather than having layers of tracks built, as sometimes happened on her albums, this was a creation caught live on camera and features Ronstadt giving emphasis and flair to different parts of her lead vocals. It is well worth checking out to see the dynamic between Linda and her band during the creation of a track. Almost a decade later, at Motown's 25th anniversary, Ronstadt performed this with Smokey Robinson himself.

'Prisoner In Disguise' (Souther)

The first of two collaborations with J. D. Souther on the album, Ronstadt chose the title track originally recorded and released by Souther in the same year that this album came out. Souther's original track was sparse and mostly acoustic. Ronstadt worked to bring it to the next level, making it a lush lament with a sweeping orchestral arrangement that pulls at the heartstrings and blends emotional resonance with heartbreaking vocals.

To achieve this, Ronstadt once again worked with David Campbell to produce string and woodwind arrangements that carry the listener through a barren landscape populated by Ronstadt and her harmonizing vocal partner – none other than Souther himself. The flute, in particular, bears a tremendous amount of importance to the arrangement as it accentuates the emotion Ronstadt conveys with her lead vocals. The 1975 *Newsweek* review of the album compliments this song as one that is able to effectively evoke a country lament. Due to the luxury of time, we're able to analyze this song more effectively due to the growth of the popular music landscape since then. What may have been considered a country song in 1975 can be seen as a borderline Broadway tune today, as all the elements of a hit Broadway song are present, including an orchestra, a duet partner and soaring vocals that take the listener out of their element.

The song itself is a journey, as it starts with acoustic guitar and swells to a much larger proportion by the time it closes under four minutes later. This track is the last to receive the attention of Campbell, who made sure that he went out with a bang on the album. He pulls out all the orchestral stops to ensure this song, out of the four he worked on, would be the one for which he is best remembered.

As a listener, I can't help but wonder if the choice of this song for the title of the album may be a bit autobiographical for Ronstadt, as she may have started to feel imprisoned by her own fame. After the success of *Heart Like A*

Wheel, Ronstadt was a bona fide superstar and, as a consequence, could no longer live life as a semi-private person. Whilst recording this album in early 1975, she may have felt her world becoming larger and smaller by degrees, as she had to be conscious of who she was and where she went in order to live her life.

Ronstadt returned to this song in 1982 for a concert in Dallas. A delicate song, it wouldn't have been in setlists very often due to the venues Linda was playing in; cavernous concert venues are designed to amplify traditional rock instruments, rather than the softer sounds present on this track. The recording currently circulating of this version hasn't been remastered, so the backing instruments can sometimes feel a bit overpowering. Despite this, Ronstadt's vocals push through and shine, especially at the end of the song, where she can sustain longer, stronger notes more effectively in comparison to her past efforts.

'Heat Wave' (Dozier/Holland/Holland)
'Heat Wave' was the second single released on the same day as the album. Although it was originally the B-side to the first single 'Love Is A Rose', this song received significantly more airtime on the radio and Asylum recognized it was more likely to be a hit, so it switched which song was the A and which side was the B. The Martha and the Vandellas classic was only a dozen years old when Ronstadt interpreted it for herself.

Rolling Stone broke down the creation of this song in an extensive article in December 1975. The Holland-Dozier-Holland song was well-known by the time Ronstadt was touring to support *Heart Like A Wheel* and when she was playing a gig, the audience demanded a sixth encore – the band needed to pull out something. 'One of us yelled out, "'Heat Wave' in D" and we did it', Gold recalled. 'We were awfully sloppy, but the crowd really liked it. So we kept the song in our set'.

A lot of time was spent on the production of this song, especially compared to its B-side 'Love Is A Rose' that was cranked out in about an hour. In the same *Rolling Stone* article, Asher was described as liking 'things to be sort of fairly perfect' and applied that sensibility to this track. Thus, many hours were spent on this single track, which was seen as one of the album's showcases.

'We tried cutting rhythm tracks several different times', said Asher, 'each with a slightly different group of musicians. None of them sounded right. So eventually, we got down to Andrew playing drums and Kenny playing bass. Andrew is a remarkable musician, but even then just getting a bass and drum track took a few days to do'.

In another contrast with its B-side, different layers were added to this track in order to construct it. Gold played multiple instruments on the song and recorded each separately, allowing him and Asher to stack them on top of one another to achieve the correct sound. Even handclaps were recorded several times, with Asher and Gold recording themselves clapping four times, then stacking them so it sounded like eight people clapping at the same time.

Throughout this process, Ronstadt would come in to make sure that the track was meeting her standards. Only after all the instrumental tracks were recorded did she lay down her vocal. The intent, all along, was to produce a hit single; that intention panned out when the song hit number five on the *Billboard* Hot 100. As a result of its hit status, the song remained on tour setlists for years to come.

'Many Rivers To Cross' (Cliff)

Ronstadt next tackles a song written by Jimmy Cliff in 1969. It retains much of the same spiritual feel as the original while also providing Ronstadt with an opportunity to do some very high-soaring vocals. Gold's mastery of the Hammond organ is consistent throughout the song, contributing to the overall feel and emotion. The organ and Ronstadt's vocal provide the framework around which everything else in the song is built around, including the last appearance of backing vocals from Gold and Edwards on the album.

This song, which opens side two of the album, serves as a breather. It also sets the mood for the rest of the album, which is much more subdued than the songs leading up to this point. If the previous six tracks were a showcase for large-scale collaborations and production, this song established the expectation that moving forward, the rest of the album would be reserved for more intimate productions featuring large emotions on a smaller scale.

'The Sweetest Gift' (Coats)

Guest musician – Emmylou Harris: acoustic guitar, harmony vocals

This song, described by *Newsweek* in 1975 as an 'artfully naïve folk antique', was the B-side of 'Tracks Of My Tears'. Thus, it was able to reach more people who may have bought just the 45, rather than the entire album, and was intentionally chosen to showcase a contrasting style.

Linda and Emmylou Harris had worked out the harmonies for this song years before and it was natural that Linda wanted to record together with Emmylou here. Due to their close friendship, it was an easy decision to replicate the success they had on *Heart Like A Wheel* with 'I Can't Help It (If I'm Still In Love With You)'. The intimate feeling of this track is accentuated by Emmylou accompanying the duet on the acoustic guitar. After the first verse and chorus, more instrumentation is introduced. Once the song reaches the middle eight, the listener is comfortably wrapped in warm vocals and soothing mandolin, which is provided by David Grisman.

The sweetest gift of this album may be this song. The bluegrass tinge is a balm for the listener, still scorched by the album's earlier heat, and shows that Asher and Ronstadt, when collaborating, can produce extremely different sounds that resonate in completely different ways within the span of a few tracks. The astute move to bring in Emmylou for vocals contributes to the homey feel of this song; Linda and Emmylou were close friends and their harmonies show they had worked hard and long on honing the sound of their voices together. This song may have also planted the idea of a future bluegrass album in Linda's mind, as this is specifically called out in the October 1975 *Newsweek* article.

Linda and Emmylou appeared on Dolly Parton's show in 1977 and although this song had been released for two years at that point, it sounded fresh and new. All three women were friends and it was natural for Ronstadt to make a rare television appearance when asked by Parton. The addition of Dolly alongside Linda and Emmylou in the choruses gave everyone a preview of what this trio could produce when working together.

'You Tell Me I'm Falling Down' (McGarrigle/Holland)
Ronstadt returned to the songwriting of one of the McGarrigle sisters – Anna, specifically – for this next song. She also called upon her friend James Taylor for guitar duties and Maria Muldaur for harmony vocals. Taylor's pretty playing introduces the song before Linda plunges in and shares a good amount of it, harmonizing with Muldaur. This song is very much in Ronstadt's wheelhouse of contemplative, plaintive tunes that are just this side of sad. However, the core message of the song is one of independence and standing up for oneself. In that, it is a liberating song that emphasizes how Ronstadt felt about her career at this time. The lyric, 'I am exactly what I am', lays bare her belief in what she does and who she is, which is a performer comfortable in her own skin and assured of her own choices.

This song is also the last McGarrigle composition Ronstadt would record until 1982. This is not due to a loss of affection for the songs, but an indication of Ronstadt's expanding musical desires. This song may be the most sentimental on the entire album and Ronstadt puts her all into crafting nuanced, sensitive vocals to draw the listener into the lyrics. Lyrics, over all else, are what drew Ronstadt to McGarrigle songs in the first place and she also made sure to let the song tell its story, channeling what the listener should feel through her voice.

This song isn't flashy and is buried on the second side of a record that made a big splash with its opening side. Thus, it is easy to overlook its value in the larger scheme of not only the album but also Ronstadt's career. However, it is a wonderfully relaxing song to sink into. The blend of the instruments balanced with the harmonized vocals allows the listener nothing less than a toned-down experience to enjoy and savor.

'I Will Always Love You' (Parton)
Linda Ronstadt's version of this song is always doomed to live in the perpetual shadow of Dolly Parton's original version and Whitney Houston's version, which rocketed the song to its most successful place on the pop

music charts, as well as in the public consciousness. This is unfortunate, as Ronstadt does an admirable job, with guitar support provided by Andrew Gold and Dan Dugmore, the latter of whom injects the steel guitar country sound into the track in a way that makes it unforgettable. *People* magazine, in November 1975, even described the song in such a way that hailed Ronstadt's version as superior to Parton's, released a year prior. This is where we must turn for a critical analysis of the track, as any current examination of this song will always be colored by comparison to Houston's version.

So why should someone go out of their way to listen to Ronstadt's version? The reason is her vocals. The song exemplifies where Linda is in her vocal growth as she goes through the exercise of stretching her voice to the upper register for a good portion of it. It's an artifact of its time in more ways than one in this regard; not only did it exist in a pre-Houston world, and absolutely stood on its own there, but it also freezes in time an instance of Ronstadt singing in a way that was outside the norm for herself.

'Silver Blue' (Souther)

The second track on the album written by J. D. Souther; his own version wouldn't appear until a solo record a year later. Similar to 'Prisoner In Disguise', Souther appears as a harmonizing vocalist for Ronstadt throughout this song. Both Souther songs were described by *Newsweek* as 'languorous, finely shaded country laments'. Perhaps more than that previous track, this shows what a great songwriter Souther was and how his words could be shaped to make a wonderful song; his songwriting abilities are probably best known due to The Eagles recording several hits written by him. Between Ronstadt and Asher, they made a beautiful arrangement that took the raw material offered by Souther and shaped it into a soft, melodic song leaking with emotion.

There's no real rocket science behind the track. Asher and Ronstadt keep the production minimal and allow subdued instrumentation, including drums, to set the stage for a powerful vocal resonance that provides closure. Ronstadt doesn't need to pull out any vocal acrobatics in such a song, as she makes it sound like it was made for her and her alone. Ronstadt's vocals, both on their own and in harmony, are a capstone experience on the record.

Hasten Down The Wind (1976)

Personnel:
Linda Ronstadt: lead vocals, backing vocals, handclaps
Andrew Gold: acoustic piano, organ, ARP String Ensemble, acoustic guitar, finger cymbal, backing vocals, electric piano, sleigh bells, handclaps, electric guitar, bass guitar, harmony vocals, tambourine, lead guitar, rhythm guitar, cowbell, clavinet
Clarence McDonald: acoustic piano
Dan Dugmore: electric guitar, steel guitar
Waddy Wachtel: electric guitar, acoustic guitar, 'reggae' lead guitar
Kenny Edwards: bass guitar, backing vocals, mandolin, string arrangements, acoustic guitar, harmony vocals
Mike Botts: drums
Russ Kunkel: drums
Peter Asher: handclaps, shaker tambourine, woodblock, cowbell, backing vocals
David Campbell: string arrangements and conductor
Charles Veal: concertmaster, violin, viola
Dennis Karmazyn: cello
Ken Yerke: violin
Richard Feves: double bass
Paul Polivnick: viola
Karla Bonoff: backing vocals
Wendy Waldman: backing vocals
Don Henley: harmony vocals
Herb Pedersen: backing vocals
Pat Henderson: backing vocals, choir vocals
Becky Louis: backing vocals, choir vocals
Sherlie Matthews: backing vocals, choir vocals
Gerald Garrett: choir vocals
Jim Gilstrap: choir vocals
Ron Hicklan: choir vocals
Clydie King: choir vocals
Bill Thedford: choir vocals
Produced at Sound Factory, March 1976 by Peter Asher
Release date: August 1976
Highest chart places: US: 3, UK: 32
Running time: 41:23

Hasten Down The Wind continued to capitalize on the public's fervor for Linda Ronstadt and her music, becoming the third album to go platinum. It also won her the Grammy for Best Pop Vocal Performance, Female at the 1977 awards show. After being presented with the award by Paul Williams and Ringo Starr, her acceptance speech was short: 'I'd especially like to thank Peter Asher, thank you'. This is in line with Ronstadt's views on awards, as she articulated to Cameron Crowe in a *Rolling Stone* interview from December 1976: 'My attitude is, "Don't give me an award, send me money". I know how good or bad I am. An award won't convince me that a record that I didn't think was good is good'.

As Crowe told it in that same article, 'The overwhelming popularity of Linda Ronstadt has caught more than a few people by surprise. For six years and four albums, she was regarded as no more than a barefoot, braless, pleasant-sounding country-ballad singer'. That a singer could mature was something people hadn't considered prior to her breakthrough album in 1974, but they couldn't help but notice it by this point. Writing for *Creem* magazine, Carl Arrington said, 'These days, she seems to be enjoying the post-cheesecake challenge of developing musically. Not only has she proven that her vocals are no studio trick, but she has now made her debut as a songsmith as well as an interpreter'. Ronstadt was very proud of this album, telling Arrington, 'I think it's the best album we've made. It has more of me in it than anything I've done'.

Even before listeners had a chance to hear what others were talking about, they were confronted with the most astounding album cover Ronstadt has released to date. Aside from the name of the album and her own name, the entire cover was devoted to a singular photograph of Ronstadt on the beach, taken by Ethan Russell. Kosh returned to put the album package together, using another photograph of Ronstadt taken by Russell for the gatefold. Cameron Crowe described the cover as 'softly erotic', while Fred Schruers described it as '...dreamily moonlit, lace by-the-sea...' in an article from the early 1980s.

'Lose Again' (Bonoff)

A power ballad if there ever was one, Linda opens up this album with the sweeping sort of track for which she had become known. Every sort of instrument was thrown in to make it a grandiose declaration of what the listener could expect from the album as a whole. The tune was written by up-and-coming singer-songwriter Karla Bonoff, who would become a good friend of Ronstadt's. Although Carl Arrington, in the December 1976 issue of *Creem* magazine, described Bonoff as a member of the 'stable of light heavyweights' Ronstadt turned to for musical inspiration, this song is a direct contradiction to that analysis. It is another example of Ronstadt's natural aptitude to choose the right song based on the lyrics, before working with Peter Asher to make it a memorable track that would stand out as the definitive version of the song in people's minds. This track was the fourth and final single released in support of the album, released in May 1977 as Ronstadt prepared to embark on a summer tour.

David Campbell returns to this album as the string arranger and conductor. It's easy to lose the strings in this song, as Dun Dugmore's guitar solo blocks out any other instrumental memory of the song. Joining Dugmore are two of the pillars of Linda's band from this time: Andrew Gold and Kenny Edwards. The four of them form not only the core of this song but also the core of the album. Ronstadt's vocals are soaring and powerful here, reaching a crescendo in the last chorus.

A promotional video was filmed for this track and, much in the same vein as 'Tracks Of My Tears' from *Prisoner In Disguise*, it provides a unique live recording from the studio. In fact, it appears as if both videos were filmed at the same time, as Ronstadt is wearing the same outfit. If anything, it shows the development of the song as it headed towards the album's final version. Ronstadt's vocals are a bit more emotionally raw here, highlighting the power of her voice as she puts it to great use at different inflection points in the song. At the close of the video, we see Linda having a moment to take in the silence following her performance as the picture fades to black.

'The Tattler' (Cooder/Titelman/Phillips)

This song originated as a gospel blues song in the late 1920s but was rearranged and reinterpreted by Ry Cooder on an album released two years prior to this one. Ronstadt saw the fun and playful tune as one that would fit in with her style and decided to record a version for her own album, following Cooder's arrangement. Much like the album immediately preceding it, *Hasten Down The Wind* is an eclectic mix that gives the public a wide swath of influences and styles to enjoy, and this track is very different from the one immediately preceding it.

The story of marriage is laid out in the song and may have reflected Ronstadt's own views on the institution. The various issues with the partner one may marry are explored, with the chorus suggesting that if both partners in a relationship try their best, they can achieve 'sweet harmony'. This is the sort of song Linda and her band could have fun with, as they layered in many different types of percussive sounds in accordance with Asher's production, including sleigh bells, shakers and hand claps. The production of the album, in this regard, is very much in line with the standards of the time as different tracks are layered together to achieve a very full, slick-sounding track.

'If He's Ever Near' (Bonoff)

The second Bonoff song for the album is another ballad that is epic in nature and weaves a tale with the assistance of Bonoff herself, as well as Wendy Waldman, contributing background vocals alongside Ronstadt. The contemplation embedded into this track could easily be taken for a spiritual meditation on a higher power, although the core of the song is someone seeking their partner in life and ultimately giving up on the active search, instead resolving to the hope that he's in her immediate vicinity. The narrator of this song had experienced what she thought was true love once, but her partner failed her and she was set adrift in the search for her soulmate.

The ethereal background vocals set this airy tune apart from others of its ilk on this album. Her band play a subdued role in the sound of this song, with most of the attention being given to Andrew Gold's organ playing, once again making this song feel more spiritual than temporal. The effective interpretation of this song, along with Asher's deft production of the number, makes it a light-feeling, beautiful midpoint for the first side of the record.

'That'll Be The Day' (Allison/Holly/Petty)
Running back to the roots of rock 'n' roll, Ronstadt and gang tear into this rousing rendition of a Buddy Holly classic. It shatters the tranquility established by the previous track with Ronstadt's opening line of 'Welllllllll…'. While the previous three tracks would most likely have been unknown to the wider record-buying public, this song was extremely known and popular. To capitalize on this, the track was released as the lead single from the album, reaching number 11 on the US pop charts and number 27 on the country charts.

The song gives the band a chance to cut loose and have fun with a song by an artist that, by and large, was idolized by many of their generation. Everyone from The Beatles to Elton John had cited Holly as a huge inspiration, and getting to cut a track written by him with as powerful a singer as Ronstadt was the opportunity they needed to show that, although they were experts at doling out ballads to the masses, they could flip on a dime and do a rock song just as well. The song serves as a wake-up call and is the right way to make the middle of an album electric. The joy, evident in Ronstadt's voice and the band's playing, can be heard as they tear through this barnburner of a track that sweeps through like wildfire and has the listener singing along the entire way.

'Lo Siento Mi Vida' (Ronstadt/Edwards/Ronstadt)
This track represents a huge rarity in Linda Ronstadt's entire catalog, as she played a hand in writing this song. In fact, alongside her father Gilbert and Kenny Edwards, she wrote this song in its entirety. This is also Ronstadt's first foray into a traditional Mexican arrangement for a song long before she released an entire album of Spanish-language songs more than a decade after this release. The English translation for this song is 'I'm Sorry My Love' and, as such, is in comfortable ballad territory for Ronstadt. There is an English verse in the middle of the song that allows Linda to belt out her notes and show a stronger side to the vocals, which had been more of a subdued Spanish lament leading up to and following it.

'We were just playing around one day and decided to write a song. In Spanish, no less', Ronstadt told *Creem* magazine in December 1976:

> We wrote a couple of lines and then thought we were real cool, saying 'Oh yeah, we're writing a song in Spanish'. When we finally got into the studio, I got my dad to come down and translate it for us. He knocked it out in about 20 minutes, then stuck around to help us get the right Mexican flavor.

This beautiful song returns to the low-key mellowness experienced at the beginning of the record with its dreamy sensibility. Ronstadt's commitment to recording a song almost entirely in Spanish foretells where her interests would take her beyond traditional pop records. Although she wouldn't break the pop mold until 1983's *What's New*, she was plotting how she could increase her record sales and popularity to go where she wanted as an artist.

'Hasten Down The Wind' (Zevon)
Arrington described this as another one of the 'light heavyweights' in his *Creem* article. Warren Zevon wasn't really well-known outside of certain musical circles at the time Ronstadt was selecting material for this record, but she identified this track as worthy. The song is about the end of a relationship and both partners realizing that the good times were in the past. This title track closes out the first side of the album. In her memoir, Ronstadt acknowledges that this is the type of track that had to be slipped into the album between songs that could be played live on stage. A song like this, she said, couldn't survive the acoustics of the arenas she was now playing when on tour.

For harmonies on this song, Ronstadt appointed Don Henley, someone who had been in her band years prior. Henley and The Eagles were recording an album of their own at the same time Ronstadt was recording this one, so he was off the road and able to swing by to contribute. The Eagles were recording *Hotel California*, which would go on to become one of the best-selling albums of all time. Henley's voice is in prime form and his harmonizing with Ronstadt highlights their mutual ability to switch from their rock voices to something soft and contemplative. Ronstadt was used to this, but Henley would have less of a chance to sing in a mellower style as The Eagles became known more and more for pure rock songs.

'Rivers Of Babylon' (Dowe/McNaughton)
This song had been performed and developed on the road prior to being chosen for inclusion on an album. In Ronstadt's words to a concert crowd in late 1975, she described the song as 'a sort of bluegrass gospel song'. The arrangement from touring to recording in the studio didn't change; it was an acapella song delivered ably by Ronstadt, Gold and Edwards with no instrumental backing. When you have perfect harmony, there's little else you need on some tracks. The choice to open up the second half of the album with this song gives the listener a chance to appreciate the voices they are familiar with, but in their purest form – bare and unaccompanied.

The song was originally released by the Jamaican reggae group The Melodians in 1970 and the lyrics draw upon psalms from the Hebrew Bible. This track also serves as a reggae appetizer for the song that follows.

'Give One Heart' (Hall/Hall)

While the prior track may have been a light attempt at reggae, this song gives Linda and her band the chance to dip their toes further into those waters. Written by John and Johanna Hall, they had written songs for his band Orleans prior to this, including 'Dance With Me'; at the time Ronstadt was recording this album, Orleans was cutting another track written by the duo, 'Still The One'. Thus, Linda would have confidence in the ability of this duo to write an effective song that she could interpret. Between very standard reggae-sounding choruses, Linda weaves her verses to tell the story of how love can be understood and how it can impact someone's life.

Reggae was something she and the band were passionate about at this time. She spoke with the magazine *Stereo Review* in November 1976 about this and how, in particular, the political bent of reggae music was attractive. Regarding the genre overall, she said, 'Our whole band is reggae crazy'. Despite their own fandom of the music style, this remains the only true reggae tribute that they put together on any of the albums that Linda released. Thus, this track represents another rarity in the Ronstadt catalog.

'Try Me Again' (Ronstadt/Gold)

This is another rarity in that this is a Ronstadt composition. Taking co-writing duties on this one is Andrew Gold, and in combination with Peter Asher, they turn this song into a tragic masterpiece. David Campbell's touch can be felt from the opening notes as his string arrangement is the total mood setter for everything about to unfold.

In an interview before a London concert as part of the tour to promote this album, Ronstadt sat down with *The Guardian* in November 1976: 'I was driving in the car, and the first song just came out', said Linda, describing the genesis of this song, 'It popped out like toothpaste – blurt! It was like dreaming in symbols, and I had no real control over it'. Talking a bit more about the background and actual writing of the song to Carl Allington of *Creem* magazine, Linda continued, 'I broke up with this guy and was driving around and then talked to my friends and got all bummed out. The next day, it just came to me in my car and I just pulled over and wrote it on the back of a parking ticket'.

While recording this song was a moment of cathartic creativity, a year later, she wasn't so keen on performing the song live. 'It's too revealing of my feelings', she shared with John Rockwell of *New Times* magazine, 'It's embarrassing to tell everybody I felt that bad. It makes my face red'. Such transparency may have been a leading factor in why Ronstadt wasn't interested in original compositions. While she was able to pour emotion into her interpretation of songs penned by other artists, she was able to keep her personal life away from her music. With this track, she may have felt she was exposed and didn't want that to be a part of her public persona.

'Crazy' (Nelson)
Tackling a Patsy Cline song, written by Willie Nelson, was next on Ronstadt's list. Two titans of the country world, Linda returned to her country rock roots with a stunning rendition of this work made famous a decade and a half prior. The tinkling piano of Clarence McDonald gives a path for Linda to follow with her vocals. The result is a gorgeous version of a country classic that stands on its own.

The public were hungry for this song, with it being described glowingly by the review press at the time of its release. In February 1977, some three months after this song was released as the third single to support the album, *Time* magazine showered her version with praise: 'She goes up against the memory of Patsy Cline's recording of Willie Nelson's 'Crazy'. Cline's version was said to be definitive. It pales next to Ronstadt's'. As she toured in the summer of 1977, this song was still on her setlist. 'The wonderfully subtle, sensuous way she sang Willie Nelson's 'Crazy' on this summer's tour owed something to Don Grolnick's elegant piano playing, but even more to her sheer absorption in a song she dearly loves', wrote John Rockwell of *New Times* magazine.

'Down So Low' (Nelson)
While 'Rivers Of Babylon' may have utilized words from the Bible and 'If He's Ever Near' evoked spiritual imagery, this is the most soulful track on the album. Written by Tracy Nelson, a blues singer, and originally published in 1968, Ronstadt and Asher arranged it to have the backing of a full choir to emphasize Linda's words and emotions. At its core, Ronstadt assumes the role of someone after a breakup who isn't successful in finding someone to replace her lost love. The vocal performance of all involved is the centerpiece of this track and the richness given by the choir can't be overstated, as it elevates Ronstadt's tribulations to the heights of a tragedy.

'Someone To Lay Down Beside Me' (Bonoff)
Linda chose a third and final song by Karla Bonoff to end the album; Bonoff's compositions bookend the listener experience. Similar to the second Bonoff song on the album, she and Wendy Waldman join Ronstadt on backing vocals. It's a song about a woman feeling the right to reject flirtatious dalliances and making the best decision for herself, something Ronstadt would increasingly become known for in her professional life (and some she had already made, such as having a producer and manager she was not in a personal relationship with; prior to Asher, Ronstadt had previously been in personal relationships with all of her former producers). The resounding message Linda makes is that she is in control, not any random person who tries to flatter her, and that others should feel empowered to be the same way. The haunting vocals and resounding words make this a great way to end an album that shows off the very best of Ronstadt during this time.

Above: Linda in the midst of her 1970s pop-rock success in Amsterdam, 1976. (*Gijsbert Hankeroot*)

Left: Ronstadt's first solo album *Hand Sown, Home Grown* was not the success she hoped it to be. (*Capitol Records*)

Right: The cover for *Silk Purse* was Linda's idea. 'I got away with more of my ideas than a lot of people did'. (*Capitol Records*)

Left: Despite being backed by the band that would become The Eagles on this record, Ronstadt's self-titled album failed critically and in sales. (*Capitol Records*)

Right: *Don't Cry Now* took three producers, over $150,000 and over a year to come out. (*Asylum Records*)

Left: *Heart Like A Wheel* was Ronstadt's breakthrough album and launched her into the superstar stratosphere. (*Capitol Records*)

Right: *Prisoner In Disguise* made Linda the first female artist to have back-to-back platinum albums. (*Asylum Records*)

Above: Glenn Frey stayed close friends with Ronstadt, even after he and his bandmates split to form The Eagles. (*Richard E. Aaron*)
Below: Dan Fogelberg, Ronstadt and members of The Eagles with California Governor Jerry Brown at a Maryland benefit for his presidential campaign, 1976. (*Karin Vismara/ Amamy*)

Above: Andrew Gold, Linda and Kenny Edwards harmonize while recording one of her classic tracks.

Below: Linda, in her classic Scout outfit she wore while touring, and her band in Los Angeles, 1977. (*Steve Schapiro*)

Left: Ronstadt with manager and producer Peter Asher, 1976. (*Ron Galella Collection*)

Below: Peter Asher's desire for 'things to be sort of fairly perfect' matched Linda's own high expectations for her records. (*Michael Putland*)

Right: Andrew Gold's contributions as a multi-instrumentalist earned him the respect of Ronstadt. (*Jim Shea*)

Below: Linda's interpretations of J. D. Souther's songs are found throughout albums she recorded in the 1970s. (*Linda Ronstadt*)

Left: *Hasten Down The Wind* won Ronstadt the Grammy for Best Pop Vocal Performance, Female in 1977. (*Asylum Records*)

Right: *Simple Dreams* knocked Fleetwood Mac's *Rumours* from the top spot on the *Billboard* album chart and sold more than 3 million copies. (*Asylum Records*)

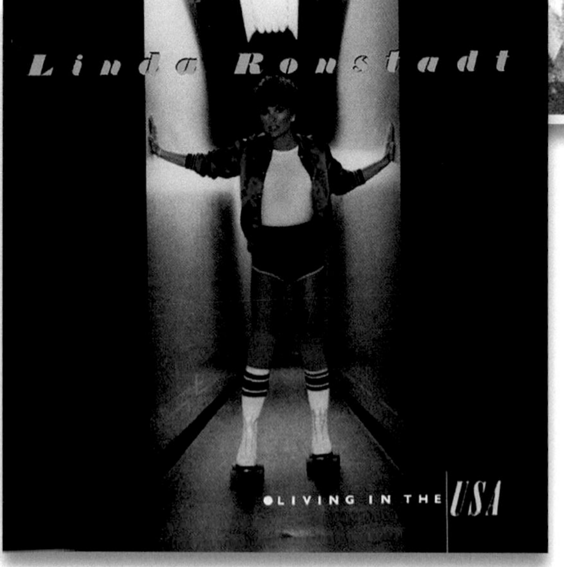

Left: *Living In The USA* shipped double platinum, meaning two million records were ordered before a single track hit the airwaves. (*Asylum Records*)

Right: *Mad Love*'s album cover was the result of the photographer giving her 'a couple of rolls of quarters and she dialed her then-boyfriend [Governor] Jerry Brown'. (*Asylum Records*)

Left: *Get Closer* was produced to finish Ronstadt's first contract with Asylum. (*Asylum Records*)

Right: Linda made a bold move with the release of *What's New*, full of songs from the Great American Songbook. (*Asylum Records*)

Left: Ronstadt's vocal training for *The Pirates Of Penzance* opened up musical possibilities that she never imagined she could reach. (*Everett Collection*)

Below: Linda put her music career on pause as she pursued her Broadway dream, pairing with the dreamy Rex Smith in *Pirates*. (*Rex Smith/Alamy*)

Right: Linda Ronstadt and Nelson Riddle worked in tandem to bring three albums of jazz standards to life. (*Ron Galella Collection*)

Below: The decision to tackle the Great American Songbook paid off for both Ronstadt and Riddle, pictured here at the ASCAP awards.

Left: Kosh's innovative album design for *Lush Life* earned him a Grammy Award for Best Album Package. (*Asylum Records*)

Right: Riddle passed away in the midst of recording *For Sentimental Reasons*. 'Some of the musicians were in tears', said Ronstadt. (*Asylum Records*)

Left: *Trio* was the album that longtime fans of Ronstadt, Parton and Harris had been waiting patiently for since it was rumored almost a decade prior. (*Warner Bros. Nashville*)

Right: Ronstadt took another risk – which paid off big time – by recording an album fully in Spanish. *Canciones De Mi Padre* sold over two million copies. (*Elektra/Asylum Records*)

Left: Featuring Aaron Neville, *Cry Like A Rainstorm, Howl Like The Wind* represents 20 years of solo experience and prowess from Ronstadt. (*Elektra Records*)

Right: Ronstadt's *Live In Hollywood* album features live tracks taken from an HBO television special filmed around the time of the *Mad Love* release. (*Rhino*)

Above: *Take Me To Your Leader.* Influenced by the psychedelic covers of Ozric Tentacles, a bemused rabbit and peahen look on. (*Hawk*)

Below: The genesis of *Trio* goes back to the late 1970s when the three women tried to make magic happen in too little time. (*Zuma Press/Alamy*)

Above: 'Kate and Anna opened a door for me and I scooted through it as fast as I could', Ronstadt wrote about the McGarrigle sisters. She is pictured here with Anna. (*Everett Collection/Alamy*)
Below: Longtime friends (and, coincidentally, both managed by Peter Asher) Ronstadt and James Taylor singing together on a 1981 Japanese tour. (*Koh Hasebe*)

Above: 'Linda is able to express multiple emotions in a single phrase, snarling out one word and crying another', wrote *Rolling Stones*' Ben Fong-Torres. (*Associated Press*)

John Rockwell, in an essay originally published in 1978, asserted that this was a watershed moment for Linda and was her way of making a bold claim through her music, even going so far as to cite it as one of a number of artistic breakthroughs Ronstadt made, beginning with this album and continuing onto the next couple. The listening public agreed as it rose to number 42 on the US pop chart as a result of it being the second single released in support of the album.

Simple Dreams (1977)

Personnel:
Linda Ronstadt: lead vocals, backing vocals, acoustic guitar, arrangements
Dan Dugmore: acoustic guitar, steel guitar, electric guitar
Waddy Wachtel: electric guitar, backing vocals, acoustic guitar, slide guitar solo
Mike Auldridge: dobro
Don Grolnick: clavinet, organ, electric piano, acoustic piano
Kenny Edwards: bass guitar, backing vocals, mandolin
Rick Marotta: drums, syndrums, shaker, cowbell
Steve Forman: marimba
Peter Asher: backing vocals, tambourine, maracas
David Campbell: string arrangements, viola
Dennis Karmazyn: cello
Charles Veal: violin
Richard Feves: double bass
Produced at Sound Factory between 23 May and 22 July 1977 by Peter Asher
Release date: 5 September 1977
Highest chart places: US: 1, UK: 15
Running time: 31:49

Linda Ronstadt continued her remarkable career success and gave her fans an album that not only performed well on the album charts but spawned five singles (half of the tracks on the album). In fact, this album holds the distinction of knocking Fleetwood Mac's *Rumours* from the top spot on the *Billboard* album chart; she also took over the top spot on the country album chart, dislodging the recently deceased Elvis Presley from his reign over there. With feats such as those, it should come as no surprise that this album went platinum. In fact, in less than a year's time, *Simple Dreams* sold over three million copies. The public's appetite for Ronstadt was insatiable.

Ronstadt, a superstar by this time, carefully controlled her image and drew a clear delineation between her private and public life. Although gossip magazines were filled with accounts of who she may be romantically involved with, Ronstadt almost never commented on such things in public. Instead, she channeled her energy into her public persona: 'I don't ever sing anything that isn't personal', Linda told John Rockwell:

> I can only sing about my own emotions, and I always wear my emotions pretty close to the surface. I don't know how to live any other way. My image is focused because I've not, on many occasions, stepped too far out of character. I don't do things that aren't authentically me. Anything I feel is not authentic gives me a headache. Even if I stumble, it's still authentically me stumbling.

Having learned her lesson while recording a song she co-wrote on the prior album, Ronstadt stuck with interpreting the lyrics of other writers. Thus, while she was still singing songs very close and personal to how she was feeling, she wasn't necessarily revealing what may or may not be happening in her own life due to the mistake of writing the lyrics herself. She was able to sing to the mood, rather than the facts, in a way that allowed her to still communicate her feelings.

The original concept for the album cover was too revealing, so Ronstadt mandated it be changed. Artificial visual obstructions were added to diffuse the appearance of Linda, dressed in only a robe, seated before a dressing table in a backstage environment. Despite straying from the original concept, the album package won a Grammy for Kosh, whose efforts once again made the album visually appealing and artistic.

She closed out her interview with Rockwell for his article in the 14 October 1977 issue of *New Times* with:

> Lots of times, I've felt I haven't gotten enough credit for the arrangements; lots of times, I feel I haven't taken enough responsibility. What I did on this album was pick the musicians, pick the tunes, pick the style of the arrangements and then just let everybody do their job, and it all worked. I think *Simple Dreams* is a great statement about California music.

'It's So Easy' (Holly/Petty)

Learning from the success of 'That'll Be The Day' on the prior album, Ronstadt chose this Buddy Holly classic to open with, giving the listeners a traditional rock song to enjoy. It's a tactic she employed on this and the following album to draw in casual listeners and convince them to stay for the duration – as if anyone who bought the album needed much convincing. The song was released as the second of five singles from the album and reached number five on the *Billboard* Hot 100. With the success of this single, as well as the lead single from the album ('Blue Bayou'), Ronstadt made pop music history by becoming the first act since The Beatles to have two singles in the Top Five at the same time. This was also groundbreaking in that she was the first woman to do this. Being the first in this regard meant that all the women who followed would necessarily bask in the shade of Ronstadt's success. Ronstadt's growl gives this song a rock edge that makes for a fantastic opening track to the album.

Billed as the 'official music video', Rhino has a live performance of this song posted on their YouTube channel. Coming from the tour to support this album, you can see how Ronstadt performed the song in front of a stadium audience and how she and her band members worked together to make it an energetic, fun number to enjoy.

In a rare sight, Peter Asher is on video providing backing vocals for the song alongside Waddy Wachtel. Seeing a live video like this makes Ronstadt fans yearn for a full concert video release, preferably with remastered sound and video.

'Carmelita' (Zevon)
The first of two Warren Zevon-penned tracks on the album, Ronstadt returns to his work to interpret a song about a junkie who needs their next fix. While those who knew Ronstadt's reputation would never have believed she could be addicted to heroin herself, her authentic delivery makes the listener fully invested in the way she articulates the lyrics in such a believable way. Don Grolnick's organ work makes this track stand out on the album, as it cascades and crescendos alongside Ronstadt to punctuate the roiling feelings the singer is professing. For a song with such serious subject matter, it is a pleasant listen and serves as a cooling-off period after the guitar-heavy 'It's So Easy'.

'Simple Man, Simple Dream' (Souther)
Ronstadt returns to a frequent contributor with this J. D. Souther song. Souther was a prolific and busy songwriter on the California scene at this time, as he was also constantly producing songs for The Eagles. Although his name may not be the best known, in terms of songwriting, in the current day, he was responsible for a string of hits for those in the California country rock scene and had a knack for producing songs that seemed tailored for those who interpreted them.

This song features the last appearance on a 1970s Ronstadt album by David Campbell, arranging the strings as he had on several past albums of hers. This is the only track on the album with something that had been a sort of go-to for Ronstadt since her Stone Poneys days – a lush orchestral track in the midst of country, rock and pop tracks. The use of this device really helped distinguish her albums from her contemporaries, as the blend of everything appealed to a very wide fan base. Dan Dugmore's steel guitar break in the middle of the song adds to the mournful tone of this straightforward ballad. Ronstadt's performance is subdued as she sings the lamenting lyrics. 'Truth is simple but seldom ever seen' is a plain sentiment and Linda may have chosen this song to follow the preceding 'Carmelita' due to its accessibility, while the larger meaning behind 'Carmelita' may not have been apparent to some listeners.

'Sorrow Lives Here' (Kaz)
This is the type of song that Ronstadt had found great success with since the onset of her solo career. The lyrics and arrangement of the song bring to mind several others stretching back to 'Long, Long Time' and evoke the same type of tragic sadness that she channels so well. Don Grolnick makes the acoustic piano's role essential here and it's hard to imagine Linda bringing a listener to tears without his deft work on the ivories. Written by Eric Kaz, who Ronstadt had turned to for material before and would return to again at the end of the following decade.

On the album, this track is the second of three slow songs to round out the first side. Overall, this album is more downbeat than the ones immediately following it. The idea behind the first side of this record is, to take a phrase from Ronstadt's friends, to 'take it easy'.

This is another one of those songs that not only gives listeners some breathing room while playing the album but also helped Ronstadt with the pace of her live shows. By selecting this mournful ballad for her album and subsequent setlists, she was able to break up the show so it wasn't back-to-back loud rock songs. This would appease longtime fans of hers, who loved Linda's ability to channel emotions into appealing ballads, as well as new fans, who would be able to appreciate her voice in a different context other than just on those songs they heard on Top 40 radio.

'I Never Will Marry' (traditional)

Guest musician – Dolly Parton: harmony vocals

The first of two traditional songs Ronstadt chose for this album, the material was familiar to her for many years prior to its appearance on vinyl. Ronstadt's first public performance of this song, which may have been the first time that future fans saw her, was on *The Johnny Cash Show* in 1969. Fresh off her time with The Stone Poneys, this was the period when she was trying to establish herself as a solo star. Ronstadt and Cash trade vocals on the show and the arrangement is a bit different from the version Linda would eventually record. As it was Cash's show, this early performance is much more country-inflected with a tinge of folk, whilst the addition of strings in the background lends it a bit more depth and beauty.

Almost a decade later, Ronstadt had the freedom to choose her arrangement for the track and decided to play with the lyrics and music. Ronstadt is credited as arranging both traditional tracks on the album, so she played a highly influential role in working them over for a record-buying audience. Rather than sing the tragic lyrics of a woman drowning, featured in the Cash performance, Linda chose to focus on lyrics centering on a woman's experience being jilted by her lover. Ronstadt brought in her friend Dolly Parton to provide harmony vocals; their duet sounds full despite their voices only being accompanied by Mike Auldridge on the dobro and Ronstadt herself on the acoustic guitar. It's a beautiful, simple country tune that somehow seems miles more modern than Ronstadt's performance with Cash. It was the album's fifth and final single, which had success on the country chart.

Linda, along with Emmylou Harris, appeared together on Dolly Parton's television show. As Ronstadt told *Hit Parader* in 1978, she was warming up backstage and playing around with this song:

> I began figuring out new chords for it and since I was there in Nashville, and it's like an old-timey sort of song, I kept hearing Dolly's voice on it. When I was getting ready to record it, I heard that she was in [Los Angeles, where Ronstadt was recording]. Her producer called me up and asked me if I would come over and sing back-up on Herbie Pedersen's album along

> with Dolly. When I saw her there, I said, 'You know, we had a lot of fun when we sang together – you should come over and sing the harmony on my record 'cause I've always heard your voice on it'. And she said that she'd love to. I really had to get up my nerve to ask her. She came over and we did the whole thing live – she just sat there in the room and I played guitar. It really made me feel good.

Whilst some songs were produced heavily, Ronstadt relied upon simpler arrangements to pull off an effective sound with minimal studio time needed.

'Blue Bayou' (Orbison/Melson)
Guest musician – Don Henley: backing vocals
One of the best-known songs by Ronstadt, this shared the record with 'It's So Easy' in the aforementioned *Billboard* feat of having two singles in the Top Five at the same time. So what made this song such an indelible hit that has lasted through the decades? A large part of it, of course, is Ronstadt's delivery of the material. As usual, her enthusiasm for interpreting a song shines through, with careful consideration given to the emphasis and emotion applied to each syllable. Ronstadt, always a perfectionist, was able to utilize studio technology to lay down a pristine vocal track that satisfied herself and the record company. This may have involved several takes in order for her to get what she considered to be the right sound.

Beyond Linda's vocal contributions, many factors combined to make this song a hit. Waddy Wachtel provides a subtle acoustic guitar, while Dan Dugmore does wonders with the steel guitar break in the middle of the song. Linda brought in one of her former bandmates to provide backing vocals; Don Henley took a break from his schedule with The Eagles to contribute to the track. As usual, with any Ronstadt album, she and Asher brought in folks for each specific track, depending on that track's needs. Even Rick Marotta, who played drums for most of the album, was asked to pull double duty and provided shaker for this song. The blend of everything together was distilled and the essence of it all created a hit. The song rose to number three on the *Billboard* Hot 100 and was nominated for the Grammy Award for Record of the Year and for Best Female Pop Vocal Performance; although Ronstadt won neither award, being nominated for two of the top awards due to this song showed its power and widespread influence.

In another preview of her career trajectory, Ronstadt recorded a version of this song entirely in Spanish, backed by 'Lo Siento Mi Vida' from *Hasten Down The Wind*. When performing this song in concert, she would frequently sing the last verse in Spanish – an excellent example of this can be heard on the *Live In Hollywood* album. The effortless way in which Linda switches from one language to another previewed her future mastery of singing in Spanish and was a way for her to explore the language through song prior to committing to a full album in that language.

The recording of this song also provided success for the artist who first released it and co-wrote the English lyrics: Roy Orbison. The renewed interest in Orbison resuscitated his career from a stagnant point since his most successful years in the prior decade. 'I think the renaissance started with Linda Ronstadt recording 'Blue Bayou', which wasn't even the A-side in America', he is quoted as saying in a biography of him. 'It sold seven to ten million for her, and I guess I felt validated or something'. Orbison's career would continue on the upswing until his untimely death in the 1980s.

While this song was to become a staple of Ronstadt concerts until she stopped touring a setlist of pop and country rock music, one of the most memorable examples of a performance came from her appearance on *The Muppet Show* in 1980. Backed by a chorus of frogs and members of Dr. Teeth's house band, The Electric Mayhem, Linda seemed a natural on the set, made to look like a magical swampland. 'The set was built to resemble Disneyland's Blue Bayou restaurant at the entrance to the Pirates of the Caribbean attraction', Ronstadt writes in her memoir, 'It was ridiculously good fun'. Many viewers, who were young at the time, consider this to be their most cherished memory of Linda Ronstadt.

'Poor Poor Pitiful Me' (Zevon)

Guest musician – Larry Hagler: backing vocals

Linda took this Warren Zevon song, reversed the gender references and made it one of her signature songs in the process. Ronstadt received Zevon's blessing to remove one of his verses and replace it with one of her own. The original verse of 'I met a girl on the Sunset Strip/She asked me if I'd beat her/She took me up to her hotel room/And wrecked my mojo heater' was replaced by 'Well I met a boy/In the Vieux Carré, down in Yokohama/He picked me up and he threw me down/Saying "Please don't hurt me, Mama!"' This was due to Linda struggling to envision herself delivering the original lyrics, as they weren't in her usual style and wouldn't be accepted by her fans.

This song was the third single from the album, dropping over three months after the album was released. It reached number 31 on the *Billboard* Hot 100 and remained on the chart for a total of nine weeks. While not wholly successful as a single, it remains a song that is closely identified with Ronstadt and receives regular play on the radio. Once again, Ronstadt's knack for picking a song to interpret led to long-term success.

Both this song and 'Blue Bayou' were pitched to Linda in a single session one night. Jackson Browne brought this song to her for consideration, while J. D. Souther was the champion of 'Blue Bayou'. As Linda reflected in her memoir, it 'was a profitable evening'.

'Maybe I'm Right' (Wachtel)

Guest musician – J. D. Souther: backing vocals

In a rare move, Linda chose a song by one of her band members to include on the album. Waddy Wachtel penned this song, the only track to really resemble the tone and feeling of those on the first side of the album. Ronstadt's delicate vocals sometimes barely make an impact on the vinyl pressing, the fragile voice seeming like it could shatter at any time. The song is an opportunity for the listener to catch their breath after two blockbuster songs where Ronstadt let her vocals loose and soar. The softness of the track is a counterpoint to the very loud, raucous tracks on either side of it.

'Tumbling Dice' (Jagger/Richards)

Already a well-known song by the time Ronstadt chose it for her album, The Rolling Stones had recorded this for their *Exile On Main St.* record a half-decade earlier. Ronstadt would rarely cover a recent hit song, but it's obvious she had an affection for the material and could have fun with it. Similar to 'Poor Poor Pitiful Me', Ronstadt reversed the gender in this song. She also changed one word in the opening line of the song from 'Women think I'm tasty, but they're always tryin' to waste me' to 'People try to rape me/Always think I'm crazy', which may be the most extreme and surprising of her lyric changes in her entire catalog. It is an aggressive way to open a song and may have been Ronstadt's way of articulating how it was different being a woman in the male-dominated world of music. By reversing the gender in this track, as well as in 'Poor Poor Pitiful Me', Linda is clearly speaking of her position in the rock world. According to an interview with John Rockwell, Linda strained her voice as she sang the final lines on the recording.

Linda worked hard at perfecting this song in the recording process. As Rockwell writes, 'It could never sound so effortlessly funky without the hours she spent on it with Jagger, with her guitarist Waddy Wachtel... and by herself, with cassettes of The Rolling Stones' studio and live versions and her own past efforts'. Ronstadt sang this song together with The Rolling Stones only once while the band was on tour in 1978 and made a stop in her hometown of Tucson, Arizona.

Ronstadt participated in the comedy concert film *FM* around the time of the recording of this album and a live version of 'Tumbling Dice' was featured on the soundtrack and in the finished film. This is a rare instance of a Linda concert performance being recorded and preserved properly, allowing the viewer to see her stage presence in full force. The energy she pours into the performance of this song is infectious and it's easy to see why concert attendees would relish the opportunity to see Ronstadt live. The combination of Linda's full-force rock growl and Wachtel's guitar solo makes this a performance well worth watching, especially now that *FM* is available in high definition. It's a terrible disappointment that more concert footage doesn't exist at such a high level of quality. Perhaps as a way to capitalize on her appearance in the movie, which was released in April 1978, Ronstadt released this as the fourth single from the album that same month. Spending eight weeks on the *Billboard* Hot 100, its highest chart position was 32.

'Old Paint' (traditional)
Guest musician – Herb Pedersen: backing vocals
The second traditional song arranged by Linda, this country song speaks to a love from her childhood: riding horses. Ronstadt would increasingly return to the formative experiences of her childhood for inspiration in her career, be it traditional Mexican music, American Songbook standards or operetta. This is a singular example of her showering affection on her love of horses and the role they had in her youth. Lovingly rendered as a homage to those days, Linda channels happy emotions into this tale of a ragged workhorse that has had a good life. The narrative structure of the song gives listeners a window into the life of a horse and its master in the American West and is a comfortable, warm way in which to close out the album.

Living In The USA (1978)

Personnel:
Linda Ronstadt: lead vocals, backing vocals
Dan Dugmore: electric guitar, pedal steel guitar
Waddy Wachtel: electric guitar, backing vocals, acoustic guitar
Don Grolnick: acoustic piano, electric piano, organ
Kenny Edwards: bass guitar, backing vocals
Russ Kunkel: drums, congas
Mike Mainieri: vibraphone, arrangements
Peter Asher: backing vocals, cowbell, tambourine, shaker, sleigh bells
David Sanborn: alto saxophone
Pat Henderson: backing vocals
Sherlie Matthews: backing vocals
Andrew Gold: backing vocals
Jim Gilstrap: backing vocals
John Lehman; backing vocals
David Lasley: backing vocals
Arnold McCuller: backing vocals
Produced at Sound Factory between 5 May and 3 July 1978 by Peter Asher
Release date: 19 September 1978
Highest chart place: US: 1, UK: 39
Running time: 35:06

This album represents the zenith of Linda Ronstadt's career in the world of contemporary pop music and, in retrospect, it can be seen as the apex of her growth from *Heart Like A Wheel* to this point. While two more pop albums would follow, they would not match the success of this album and seem more like a post-script to this part of her career rather than a continuation of her domination in the pop music or country rock fields.

The public's desire for Ronstadt's music caused this album to go double platinum before it even shipped to record stores. Advance sales were propelled by the excitement for a new album on the heels of the highly popular and successful *Simple Dreams*. Photographer Jim Shea and Kosh combined efforts to make a very memorable album cover that is a creature of its time, featuring Linda Ronstadt on roller skates. Alternative releases of the album were also available; one was pressed on red vinyl, while the other was a picture disc featuring Ronstadt lacing up her skates.

The album went all the way to the top of the *Billboard* Pop Albums chart in the United States, as well as number three on the *Billboard* Country Albums chart (despite it having almost no country flavor to it at all). The album was an unrivaled success and showed that Ronstadt was the queen of the music scene. No one could come close to her selling power and it was by this time that Ronstadt may have realized that she had the power to take her career wherever she wanted – her name would sell the albums, rather than the content. Her fans trusted her to choose excellent music and they would buy what was released under her name.

'Back In The U.S.A.' (Berry)

Ronstadt chose songs in a variety of ways; she would keep a list of songs on her and add to it when she heard something exceptional. Always on the lookout for material, she and Glenn Frey were riding around Los Angeles in his car, reflecting on how they had started from the bottom and now they were rich and famous as a result of their efforts. Frey had a mixtape in the car's tape deck and just as he and Linda were rejoicing, as well as appreciating how great it was to cruise around accompanied by such good music, this song came on. 'Boy, that would be a great song to sing. I think I'll do that one', said Ronstadt, as quoted in Marc Eliot's book *To The Limit: The Untold Story Of The Eagles*. In her mind, the song was all about how successful one could be in America and expressed the joy of living in the country.

The version Ronstadt was inspired by was recorded by its writer Chuck Berry and originally released in 1959. Berry's version was a hit and came at the height of the American rock 'n' roll era; this is the period of time that inspired so many future stars and songs like Berry's were imprinted in their memory. Ronstadt rearranged her version to fit the more modern pop style, as well as giving her voice space to breathe. It's a rollicking tune that hurtles through its runtime, so while Ronstadt kept the tempo of the original, the old-fashioned backing vocals that marked it as a quasi-doo wop song were done away with. Electric guitar and a honkytonk piano sound were kept, providing just the right touch of nostalgia here. As the first song on the album, it sets the energy standard for the entire record and was a canny pick to begin proceedings. As the lead single from the album, released the month before the album, it rose to number 16 on the *Billboard* Top 100 chart. John Rockwell, writing about her interpretation of the song, said, 'Linda's cover falls right about in the middle of her other versions of rock and rhythm-and-blues from this era. The vocal is nicely energetic, and the band matches Berry's arrangement ...'

A live recording of the song was included on Ronstadt's *Live In Hollywood* album and features a raw, growling performance from Linda as she digs into the material and has a good time performing it for the studio audience. When listening to the album and live versions back-to-back, you can appreciate how polished the studio productions had become for Ronstadt's releases. Although the difference is, of course, apparent for other releases from this live album, this may be the best example of how Ronstadt could take an album track and let loose with it when performing it on stage.

Ronstadt performed this song in 1987 alongside Berry, with Keith Richards on guitar, in celebration of Berry's 60th birthday for a televised special. The circumstances around this performance are told in Bruce Pegg's book *Brown Eyed Handsome Man: The Life And Hard Times Of Chuck Berry*. By this time, Ronstadt had honed her vocal performances after being on Broadway and performing a series of standards albums with Nelson Riddle, who tailored the arrangements to her voice. Mark Slocombe, a production assistant for the television special, said the performance of the song was practiced in the key of C. However, when the live performance began, Berry's playing mandated a change to G. 'Linda Ronstadt's such a pro, you really don't hear her strain or muff it. But ... she was so pissed off when she walked off that stage, she went right through the Green Room, right out the stage door, climbed into her limo and never came back for the second show'. For safety, a second taping was scheduled to make sure the best versions of all songs were included on the final special and the supporting album. Although Ronstadt eventually agreed to let the audio recording of the song be released, 'they had a hard time getting [Ronstadt] to sign the release for the [performance] because she was so pissed off', said Slocombe. Ronstadt held herself to a high performance standard and the change in key meant she wasn't able to give, in her opinion, her strongest performance.

'When I Grow Too Old To Dream' (Hammerstein II/Romberg)
Hints about where Ronstadt's career would go are sprinkled throughout this and other albums from the 1970s. Just as *Hasten Down The Wind* previewed her foray into traditional Mexican music, this track forecast her journey into recording standards. In 1978, no one would have imagined that within the next decade, Linda would record three full albums of standards in the vein of this song. Ronstadt would sing multiple songs by Richard Rodgers on those future standards albums, but this is the only time she would sing a song by his longtime partner Oscar Hammerstein on any of her albums. The song is tinged with sugar and is one of the sweetest Ronstadt recorded. While her later standards material leaned more towards jazz, this is a ballad that begins quietly before building steadily through Linda's voice to be a show-stopping number. Linda's voice was always strong and this song shows the potential that, in a couple of years, would be refined by Broadway training. This track seems like an outside pick for a pop album but shows an interest not previously musically expressed by Linda. As Rockwell writes, 'Apparently there was a good deal of experimentation in the studio as to just how to sing it and with what arrangement', which indicates just how unexplored this type of territory was for Ronstadt and Asher.

This is one of three songs Ronstadt sang on her appearance on *The Muppet Show*, where she had the honor of being the second-to-last guest ever in the fifth and final season. When the show was taped, in May 1980, Linda was preparing for her stint on Broadway in *The Pirates Of Penzance*. It would have been around this time that she was deep in vocal training for the part of Mabel, as she had canceled a summer tour in order to prepare and star in the operetta. The number starts with Ronstadt singing to Kermit the Frog, who was the object of her affection throughout the episode. Accompanied by Rowlf the Dog on the piano, Ronstadt weaves her way through the song as it becomes a duet with Kermit, then a company number with a large portion of the Muppet cast. Ronstadt's vocal maturity is evident here.

'Just One Look' (Carroll/Troy)

Ronstadt returned to pop music's past with this next selection, also returning to a formula listeners were familiar with from her last few albums. Linda selected a known hit from the previous decade, originally sung by Doris Troy, who was also a co-writer on the track. Choosing a song by a female singer makes this a unique song on the album; the other classic songs Linda interprets were all done by male artists.

The arrangement of the song is similar to Troy's, with the addition of Pat Henderson and Sherlie Matthews on backing vocals in addition to Ronstadt herself. Dan Dugmore and Waddy Wachtel trade-off electric guitar lead lines on the track to give it more of a rocking feel than the original version. Something that is present on both the original and Ronstadt's version, however, is a jaunty piano line that accompanies the vocals. While Troy's original is more of a shuffle, Linda's has a quicker tempo that rollicks through the track. While still respecting the original, Ronstadt is able to interpret it for a new decade. The song was the third single released from the album and peaked at number 44 on the *Billboard* Top 100 for the week ending 17 March 1979. Journalist John Rockwell wrote glowingly about this track, 'I think Linda's version is superior on every count, and not just because she has the better voice… her band plays better and is far better recorded, and the arrangement builds subtly with the addition of tambourine and cowbell'.

Appearing on the *Live In Hollywood* album, listeners (and viewers of the special) could see how this song had evolved in Ronstadt's repertoire between the recording of this album and the taping of the special in 1980. Ronstadt growls and belts the song, turning it into a positively aggressive number. You can even spot Ronstadt's longtime producer Peter Asher on cowbell duties in the background.

'Alison' (Costello)

This song marks Ronstadt's first interpretation of an Elvis Costello song. Linda sings it beautifully and really rounds out the song by bringing in David Sanborn for an evocative, sultry saxophone solo. The control Ronstadt exhibits with her voice throughout is evident as she rounds one word into another, bemoaning the fate of the titular subject. In an essay on the album, John Rockwell writes about the blend Ronstadt and Sanborn achieve together, explaining that the '…blend comes with the final syllable in the song… in which Sanborn's sax emerges as if from within Linda's last falsetto note'.

There was a bit of a dust-up from Costello's end on Ronstadt covering one of his songs. In short, he wasn't in favor of her doing one of his songs. 'I've never communicated with him directly, but I heard that someone asked him what he thought and he said he'd never heard it, but that he'd be glad to get the money', Ronstadt told *Playboy* in 1980, as she prepared to release another album with songs by him included. 'So I sent him a message: "Send me some more songs, just keep thinking about the money"'.

The public responded favorably to the song when it was released as the fifth and final single from the album, as it reached number 30 on the *Billboard* Adult Contemporary chart.

'White Rhythm & Blues' (Souther)

This is Ronstadt's last time turning to material written by J. D. Souther for an album and, appropriately, it's a slow number that closes out the side of an album. The languid way in which Linda croons the song expresses the feel of the piece and is a wonderful companion track to 'Alison'. While there is nothing really exciting about this track in particular, it serves as a set piece for the listener and keeps them in the same mood as the needle inches closer to the center of the record.

'All That You Dream' (Barrere/Payne)

Linda is able to open up the second half of her album with a thumping, rocking number that announces it's time to wake up and get ready – this was originally meant to close out the album. As side one ends with the final J.D. Souther composition, she opens this side of the album with the last number by Little Feat she would cover. The track is wide open and the guitar work by Waddy Wachtel is notable, as is the trippy slide guitar mastery by Dan Dugmore (which sounds so close to a synthesizer that it's easy to make that identifying mistake).

Ronstadt took a pretty standard, spare track from Little Feat and turned it into something even more. This is where the magic of Linda's touch is on display: 'Ronstadt sings the song with an exact yet unstudied command of pitch… and a tough, defiant persona. The toughness is reinforced by several devices; the familiar growls, slurred diction and precise touches of vocal color here and there…' writes John Rockwell, who was very impressed at how Linda was able to take the raw material of the original song and transform it into a rock number.

'Ohh Baby Baby' (Robinson/Moore)

Easily the most sultry track on the record, Ronstadt takes on a Smokey Robinson & The Miracles number. In 1965, it was a hit on both the *Billboard* Hot 100, as well as the R&B chart. David Sanborn's saxophone sets the mood for the entire track as it leads listeners toward a waiting Ronstadt, whose vocals are some of the smoothest she has ever put on record. Delicate and sexy, the whole song has an ambiance that perforated the popular music landscape and made this interpretation a hit in its own right, charting on several *Billboard* charts, including the Hot 100, Adult Contemporary, Hot Soul and even Country. This is a testament to Ronstadt's continued crossover appeal, as this song strays far from the country singles she released early in her career.

The success of this song was due, in part, to its release as the second single from the album. It was released as a single in November 1978, with the next single not being released until February 1979. Sales of this album were already spectacular before it shipped, but the large period of time between singles being released highlights the confidence that Asylum had in the single's ability to carry holiday sales of the record far beyond the typical Christmas shopping season.

Ronstadt performed this with Robinson as a duet for the Motown 25th anniversary celebration and describes her thrill at singing live with Robinson, whose work she had admired and interpreted for years. 'Smokey was unfailingly supportive and gracious, but my knees were knocking together', Linda writes in her memoir, 'Singing 'Ohh Baby Baby' while staring into Smokey's eyes was both intimidating and exhilarating and remains one of the highest peaks of my career'. High praise indeed from a legend who smashed records in her own right.

'Mohammed's Radio' (Zevon)

This album truly was one of lasts, as this is the final album on which Ronstadt would record a song written by Warren Zevon. At its core, the message of the song is about the power of the radio and song. In some ways, this is a traditional pop song that tells a linear story as it touches upon several characters and how they interact with one another and the radio in question.

Ronstadt is able to bring out her rock 'n' roll vocals on this track again, giving listeners a switch-up from the soft tones of the previous song. The backing vocals from her band give a collaborative feel that is absent from some of Ronstadt's songs, as she typically lets a track stand on its own vocally with minor backing or harmonizing vocals from others. A mid-tempo rock song, the band are able to let their instruments get a bit of a shine, too. The subdued nature of the track fits in with the second half of this record and helps shape it toward its conclusion two tracks later.

Rockwell writes of the song:

> It represents not only an overpowering piece of singing and an inspired arrangement, both far truer to the song than Zevon himself can muster, but also the first time Linda has attempted, with sovereign success, a song that transcends the humanistic, amorous-psychological basis of her music and moves into the realm of metaphorical abstraction.

This heady piece of commentary is quite complimentary of Ronstadt's interpretation, as she is proven to be up to the task of cutting through some tough material and correctly and expertly distilling its essence for the listeners.

'Blowing Away' (Kaz)
Not to be confused with 'Keep Me From Blowing Away' from a few albums prior, this song stands on its own as a significantly different composition that feels right at home in its placement on this album. Dan Dugmore once again applies his touch on the steel guitar to produce a synthesizer-like sound at the beginning of the track. Ronstadt lets her strong voice pick up the song from there and runs with it; it's tantalizing to think how this song might have sounded acapella, as Linda's voice is at its peak here and is a true hidden gem on the album.

Linda Ronstadt joined Bonnie Raitt, who recorded this song for her 1975 album *Home Plate*, at a tribute concert for the recently deceased Lowell George of Little Feat on 4 August 1979. The arrangement of this version is more stripped down and truer to Raitt's album version than Ronstadt's. As Ronstadt would later admit, she always tended to harmonize when singing with another female singer, so the combination of these two powerful singers blows it out of the water. One of the greatest missed opportunities in Ronstadt's long career is the lack of a recorded collaboration with Raitt, as this performance only exists in a poorly recorded videotaped format.

'Love Me Tender' (Presley/Matson)
Ronstadt and her band incorporated this song into their setlist shortly after Elvis Presley passed away in 1977. By the time they recorded this album almost a year later, they had honed their interpretation and were well used to it, a fact that shines through on the album version. As a result, this isn't a song they needed to work out in the studio, it was something they had played nightly for some time while on tour.

Ronstadt's inclusion of this on the album is a tribute to the influence of Presley on the American music landscape and closes out the album's loose theme of Americana and a celebration of various aspects of its music. It also fits in extremely well both as an album-ending number and the closing song of an album side that is very mellow compared to the first side. The organ work on the track is very delicate, a word that can also be applied to the track as a whole – it feels like it could shatter at any moment. The song was the fourth single from the album, released in February 1979.

An enterprising DJ paired up Ronstadt and Presley's vocals to make a duet of the two singing the song. This feels very familiar to modern ears, as Natalie Cole had great success dueting with her long-dead father in the 1990s, but this was relatively novel in the late 1970s and was a way for the two superstars to sing together. This was never officially released but can still be found online.

Bonus Track
'The Married Men' (Roche)
'Phoebe and I were in New York about a year ago and we went down to Gerdes Folk City to see the Roche sisters and we both fell in love with this

one amazing song they had written and Phoebe recorded it', said Linda, as she introduced this duet with Phoebe Snow on the 19 May 1979 episode of *Saturday Night Live*. 'I was so jealous that she got to scoop me on this great tune that I told her, [that] the only way she could make it up to me was if she let me sing it with her one time'. Ronstadt had a wide variety of friends in the industry and, at other times, spoke of her affection for Snow. This duet, done only once for SNL, showed the potential the two had together and it's befuddling that they never worked together. It's also interesting that Ronstadt never chose a song by the Roche sisters for any of her albums.

Linda and Phoebe trade lines back and forth before coming together to harmonize on the chorus. The earthy sound of Snow's voice intertwining with Ronstadt's sweet vocals is a bewitching combination. The backing band do a wonderful job subtly playing behind the two women, not interfering with the weaving vocals as they tell the story of being the other woman. At the end, both of them hit a harmonized high note as the camera pulls back. The audience applauds a once-in-a-lifetime performance and we are left to wonder what might have been had these two recorded together.

Mad Love (1980)

Personnel:
Linda Ronstadt: lead vocals, backing vocals
Bill Payne: keyboards
Michael Boddicker: synthesizers
Dan Dugmore: electric guitar, electric guitar solo on 'Mad Love'
Mark Goldenberg: electric guitar, backing vocals, electric guitar solo on 'How Do I Make You' and 'I Can't Let Go'
Danny Kortchmar: electric guitar, electric guitar solo 'Hurt So Bad'
Mike Auldridge: Dobro
Peter Bernstein: acoustic guitar
Bob Glaub: bass
Russ Kunkel: drums
Peter Asher: tambourine, percussion
Steve Forman: percussion
Waddy Wachtel: backing vocals
Nicolette Larson: backing vocals
Rosemary Butler: backing vocals
Kenny Edwards: backing vocals
Andrew Gold: backing vocals
Produced at Record One between 24 October 1979 and 10 January 1980 by Peter Asher
Release date: February 1980
Highest chart places: US: 3, UK: 65
Running time: 31:09

This album is the first of Linda Ronstadt's departures from the material she was best known for. Although the following album would be a return to form, this can be seen as Ronstadt going against the preconceived notions of her overall sound; this was an opportunity for her to find success outside of what she had already done, record company expectations be damned. Ronstadt may have seen herself as part of the industrialization of rock in the 1970s and this album was her bid to get back to what she thought was its more enjoyable roots. 'Rock 'n' roll is fun and the music is coming back', Linda told *Rolling Stone* in 1980:

> There was an enormous amount of narcissism and self-seriousness in the last ten years, which I think had to be there. And then it got detached, so it became like Devo, sort of convoluted and inward, with a real mechanical approach. Then, in order to stop being that, it all has to be kind of joyous.

New York magazine touched on this album as they caught up with Ronstadt ahead of her next project. *Mad Love* was ...

> ... a celebration of the rebarbarized rock 'n' roll of the New Wavers, stripping away the strings, overdubbing and aural enhancers that had been part of the texture of her previous albums. And on the road, she digs into this music with a new authority and power. 'I feel like I'm just learning how to do it', she says. 'It's like I finally know'.

Recording technology had advanced as the new decade began and this album was the first one Ronstadt and Asher produced digitally. As she wrote in her memoir, this allowed her to sing more effectively on her records because she could do less takes; they could insert her best vocals alongside the best instrumentation, creating a better recording experience overall. They could also take different pieces from different takes to make the best track. 'We could drop in the most microscopic segments: a breath, a final consonant, a syllable that had wavered out of tune'.

Her gamble paid off and this album went platinum and debuted at number five on the *Billboard* album chart, which was a first for a female artist and broke a record at the same time. Needless to say, Linda proved her point by straying from the format for which she was best known and gained the latitude to do what she wanted as an artist from this point forward: 'I don't think there was a conscious attempt to change. Things change imperceptibly of their own accord – in music, personalities, etc. And if you're involved in music or any occupation that exerts any influence over the culture, then your response to that has an impact – it's 50% influencing and 50% being influenced' she continued in *Rolling Stone*. It really can be seen as the start of Ronstadt's true independence as an artist as she charted her own course and proved time and again that her instincts were always on the mark – no matter the material, she would make a success out of it. In the same *Rolling Stone* article, she said:

> I went around to every club there was and I saw all the acts; I just digested it. I sat and talked to [producer] Peter Asher in his manager's hat about what I'd heard and what I wanted to do. He always encourages me to try to find another producer, but I honestly feel he's right for me. I think it shows a lot more courage and a lot more strength to try to evolve with the same team.

Mark Goldenberg, who contributed songs and played on the album, reflected on the differences in making this record and those that had come before it. In an interview with *Billboard* in 2020, he said:

> We cut those songs in fairly rapid order. Previous incarnations of her studio band featured a lot of overdubbed guitar and it was very produced, and I think Peter and Linda wanted to do something a little more immediate and more direct with just good live playing. And the stuff that we recorded – those vocals were live vocals. She didn't go back later to do any overdubs; she largely sang it while I played guitar next to her.

Photographer Peter Howe and cover designer Kosh stuck Ronstadt in a phone booth to take the iconic cover photo. As Kosh reflected in a Facebook post in celebration of the album's 40th anniversary:

> We scouted the phone booth location beforehand and worked out how to light this so Linda would look great in an urgent, grainy, noir situation. We then gave her a couple of rolls of quarters and she dialed her then-boyfriend Jerry Brown, the governor of California!! This is one of my favorite pieces: she looks fabulous, coming straight at you and it all fits the music perfectly.

The hot pink accents on the black and white photo make the album pop and grab the listener's attention immediately.

'Mad Love' (Goldenberg)
The first of three songs written by Mark Goldenberg for his band The Cretones – who were releasing their first album in the same year that this album came out – this track indicated to listeners that they were not in for the same experience they were used to with Ronstadt. 'Mad Love' is definitely a new wave track that still provides Ronstadt with the ability to break out her hard rocking voice but applied to a different style of rock. Linda's commitment to having an authentic new wave sound throughout the album is shown through her hiring of Goldenberg to arrange songs for the album, as well as to provide lead guitar for many of the tracks. This canny move again highlights Linda's ability to find unknown talent and utilize songs and styles to her advantage; this repeats something she did, for example, with Karla Bonoff a few years prior.

1980 was the advent of music video dominance, a necessity if you wanted to sell albums, as the visual medium was a facet that had yet to be exploited wholesale by the music industry. This posed a conundrum for Ronstadt, who had previously vastly limited her appearances on television and was loathe to grant interviews. However, the controlled environment of a music video set meant she was able to exert creative control of her image before it was released to the public, which also meant she was able to extend her drive for perfection to the new medium. The music video for this song features Ronstadt's new punk style, including a pixie haircut and a striped shirt below a black jacket. It appears to have been shot in an unfinished studio, with exposed insulation between raw two-by-fours. The aesthetic was in line with the new wave and punk atmosphere, which was rejecting the glamourous rock lifestyle for one that, they believed, was more authentic.

The drive for Ronstadt to strike a different path was formed, in large part, by the material she was consuming as a fan of music. Always on the lookout for a new song, she was drawn into the new wave style because it was fun to sing – Linda never really chose a song that didn't appeal to her.

At this point in her career, she had done several albums of 1970s rock that had proven effective not only in her artistry but also in her success as a musician. However, it was also an area she had been over several times. By trending more towards new-wave sounds, she was striking an unexplored path for herself. While a gamble, it gave her new material to play with and new ground to cover. The burgeoning new wave scene struck her as the next step in her own evolution and allowed her to set aside the expectations her previous material had set. Singing a song such as this was a way for her to refresh herself as an artist and gave her a new way in which to grow.

'Party Girl' (Costello)

Ronstadt's glib message asking Elvis Costello to send her songs in order to keep making him money worked, despite him making clear his displeasure towards Ronstadt's previous Costello cover. As Fran Drescher's character, Bobbi Flekman, says in *This Is Spinal Tap*, 'Money talks and bullshit walks' in the music industry and this is a key example of that within Linda's career. As the first Costello track on the album, Linda chose to sing about a woman who wanted to be known for more than just being a party girl. This may have been a subconscious choice for Ronstadt, who had been hinting at a desire to do more than just her typical rock-oriented albums for some time before this, scattering seeds of musical styles she was interested in throughout her past few albums.

This slow-tempo song gives Ronstadt's voice space to vacillate between a quiet whisper and a hard rock shout. The final note Ronstadt holds to end the song completes an aural experience that one wouldn't have expected when the song began; she is able to turn several corners throughout to keep listeners guessing.

This song, like several on the album, was performed live for an HBO special in 1980 but was cut from the album *Live In Hollywood* when that album was released in 2019. A video of the performance exists and is well worth seeking out. The tempo is slower than the album version and Linda fills it with her voice, stretching notes longer and giving free rein to the notes she clipped shorter on the album version.

'How Do I Make You' (Steinberg)

In a 2013 interview, songwriter Billy Steinberg admitted that he was going for a similar sound to the Knacks' 'My Sharona' when penning this song. Wendy Waldman, one of Linda's backup singers, brought this song to her attention via a demo Steinberg and his group Billy Thermal had cut. This came as a surprise, as Steinberg didn't know that Waldman and her boyfriend, Billy Thermal guitarist Craig Hull, would let Ronstadt listen to the demos. Steinberg would go on to achieve massive success as a songwriter in the 1980s, penning Madonna's 'Like A Virgin' and Cyndi Lauper's 'True Colors'. His first song on an album, however, was this one.

The song veers on the edge of punk and is one of the most boisterous tracks recorded by Ronstadt in this or any other era. Her rock growl is in full effect as she rockets her way through the song, daring the lead guitar to keep up with the pace she sets. Nicolette Larson provides backing vocals and her voice blends beautifully with Linda's to underscore the central question of the song. It's a wonderful party of a song. On her *Live In Hollywood* album, Ronstadt lets loose even more on the track and gets into the rock groove by practically shouting the song; it was the high-energy song for which she may have always been looking. This song was the lead single from the album and rose to number ten on the *Billboard* Hot 100. By sending this out in advance of the album, Ronstadt was making a bold statement that this is what the record-buying public could expect from the pending release. This song was nominated for the Best Rock Vocal Performance Female category at the 1981 Grammys.

'I Can't Let Go' (Taylor/Gorgoni)
Originally a hit for The Hollies in 1966, it charted high in the UK and sent a ripple over to the US charts, where it just failed to crack the Top 40. The most obvious change from that better-known version is that Ronstadt tackled it as a solo singer, whereas The Hollies as a group were able to arrange it for their multiple vocalists. However, the technology existed in 1980 to allow Ronstadt to back herself on the record, along with assists from Nicolette Larson and Rosemary Butler. Updating the arrangement from a pretty straightforward Merseybeat song, Ronstadt made the electric guitar prominent in her version, lending it almost equal stature with her own vocals which, at times, compete with one another. The third and final single from the album, it peaked at number 32 on the *Billboard* Hot 100 charts.

The version of this song on the *Live In Hollywood* album gives a window into how mixing played a part on the record but wasn't necessarily the luxury Ronstadt probably wanted when mastering the live version for release in 2019. Although she was able to work off the master recordings that had been recently unearthed, she was still unable to crank down the volume on her lead vocal – which is to the listener's benefit. Rather than fading out her last word prior to the guitar solo, the listener is able to hear and appreciate the note she clung to and boosted while going into the solo.

Linda sang the song live for quite some time, with a fan recording of a concert in 1995 showing a performance even more powerful than the one released on either record. A big component of this is the Broadway training Ronstadt underwent right after this album came out. The song was already constructed around her big voice; what she realized afterwards is that the song could expand an even more substantial lead vocal presence.

'Hurt So Bad' (Randazzo/Weinstein/Hart)
Linda chose to end the first side of the album with an interpretation of this hit by Little Anthony & The Imperials. This, along with the preceding

song, was a sort of return to her normal song selection, showcasing what listeners expected from a Linda Ronstadt album – an assortment of hits from yesteryear. In order to appease those expectations, as well as give her a known song or two to play with, Ronstadt put these two songs on the first side of the record. As it was, these were probably the last two recognizable songs on the album for her regular listeners. Side two would be filled with newer compositions and would give listeners a taste of new wave and punk.

The track from Little Anthony & The Imperials was symphonic in nature, bringing in strings and making quite a dramatic entry for a number from 1965. Linda chose to update the arrangement and make it into a new wave track that spoke to the current musical landscape in 1980. Ronstadt brought vocals reeking of desperation to the song and it simply oozed the begging and pleading she was singing about. Danny Kortchmar's electric guitar work, including a solo, only served to underscore the insistent lyrics aimed at an unseen lover. Peaking at number eight on the *Billboard* Hot 100, this was the second single from the album and was released just a month after the album itself. It also has the distinction of being the last single from Linda Ronstadt to reach the Top Ten as a solo artist.

Due to it being a single, this song also got the music video treatment. Although lit differently from the video for 'Mad Love', it was probably filmed on the same day as Ronstadt's outfit is the same, as is the set, which, upon further inspection, looks like it is supposed to be an unfinished basement. Although jamming in a basement is not outside the realm of possibility for Ronstadt at any point in her career, the feel of this music video is part of how she was shaping her image for this album. The song was also part of the set for *Live In Hollywood* and features, again, more of a focus on Ronstadt's vocals due to a different audio mix. Kortchmar's guitar also sounds different, as he was able to riff a bit each time he played the number live.

'Look Out For My Love' (Young)

Linda returns to someone familiar here, but to a song that was also new territory for that person. Alongside Ronstadt and many other prominent artists from the 70s, Neil Young was poking around the new wave scene with his version of this song. Linda had, years before, toured and sung backup for Young but decided to tackle one of his songs from his newer batch of material. Linda's arrangement gives a lot of space for the electric guitar, in line with the rest of the album. Linda's version is a striking contrast from Young's; even though the lyrics were construed as part of the new wave movement, he recorded it with an acoustic guitar, fiddle and backing vocals. Ronstadt's arrangement is a vast improvement on the original and is both more memorable and better executed.

While the song features a strong middle part, mandating a louder, more robust voice, the vast majority of it is a simpler arrangement for her voice. Ronstadt performed this during her live special in 1980 but did not select it for inclusion on her *Live In Hollywood* album that used the same recordings. It's one of the victims of both the track limit of a vinyl record, as well as Linda's desire for perfection. There must have been something that bothered her about this performance that caused her to exclude it from release, although it's hard to see what she may have disliked about it.

'Cost Of Love' (Goldenberg)
Ronstadt is able to get a bit edgy with her vocals on this track, coming off more than a little punk with how she phrases and emphasizes different parts of the narrative. This is the second track written by Goldenberg and having him around to help with the arrangement let Linda expand her performance capabilities and play with how her voice could sound on a different type of track. The way in which Linda uses her voice to try to entice the subject of the song, taunting and teasing along the way, is a change from how she typically delivered songs. Rather than singing from a hypothetical perspective, this is a very direct song and the first-person nature of the lyrics gives Ronstadt a different way in which to put over a song: with vocal jabs and a melodic chorus. The guitar almost acts as a backup singer on this track, matching her note for note in the chorus.

Curiously, although this song was not a single from the album, it received the music video treatment. In terms of setting, décor and costuming, there is no change from the previously mentioned music videos produced for the album. The song could have been possibly considered as a single for the album and then plans changed later, or they may have just wanted to film another song as long as they had the studio booked. Regardless, we are treated to another great Linda performance of a song that didn't linger around her setlist following the album's release and promotion. This was another song cut from the *Live In Hollywood* release in 2019, most likely due to the album needing to have more well-known Ronstadt hits on it to appeal to the modern audience. Linda's vocals are raw in this live performance and may be one of the only live performances we have of the song. She gives her voice an edge that is smoothed over in the *Mad Love* album cut.

'Justine' (Goldenberg)
The last Goldenberg composition on the album, Linda addresses the song's subject by using her punk voice. The song is punctuated frequently by guitar licks that guide Ronstadt to her next line; the guitar solo in the middle of the song by Dan Dugmore digs deep. The solo is more in line with the 1970s rock sensibility that Ronstadt was leaving behind; used in moderation, such as it was on this album, it made more of an impact than if it were among its peers on a whole record of similar-sounding songs. It's a song of warning to the song's subject about not being led astray by one's heart, a sentiment that, at its core, is something Linda sang about many times over the course of her career. The magic is how Ronstadt was always finding new ways in which

to deliver this message through a combination of fresh songwriting talent, new ways to vocally interpret her chosen lyrics and subverting expectations through instrumentation choices. As it is on the second side of the album, written by a relative unknown and was never a hit song, it's easy to overlook the material. However, it's another example of a hidden treasure Ronstadt purposely put on an album that not only gives her the chance to interpret it as she wants it heard but exposes the listener to something they may never have heard had it not been for her album.

'Girls Talk' (Costello)
The title of this song spoke directly to Ronstadt and perhaps her distaste for rumors swirling around her personal life. She would become more outspoken about the intrusion of the press as the decade wore on, but as she was a megastar, there were always items relating to her in magazines. Thus, when selecting material for her next album, she was drawn to it for a number of reasons; personal feelings aside, it was also an Elvis Costello composition and fit right in with the new wave theme she curated for the album. 'I like to take his songs and switch the gender around because his gender assignments are very flexible', Ronstadt told *Rolling Stone* in 1980, talking about this song in particular: 'You remember high-school girls' talk', she said:

> It's always gossipy and it's scandalous and it's naughty, and there's always some real hard kernel of truth in it. Girl's talk is something you can use to defend yourself, and you can use it to attack with – a flexible kind of weapon. I love that first line in the song: 'There are some things you can't cover up with lipstick and powder'.

Ronstadt's arrangement for the song somewhat closely followed Dave Edmunds', who first released the song in 1978. Costello's version wouldn't come out until the month following the release of *Mad Love*, leaving Linda's version sandwiched in the middle. The way Ronstadt sings through the song's narrative marks it as an achievement with the material she had chosen – her version is the best executed of the three. While the attention for the singles was primarily on older material, Ronstadt may have been better served with a song like this coming out in lieu of or in addition to one of those selections.

'Talking In The Dark' (Costello)
The last track on the album and the last selection from Costello, Ronstadt chose a jaunty song that utilizes the synthesizer for the first time ever on one of her albums. If there was any sound that defined early 1980s music, it was the synthesizer. The synthesizer was applied in a smart way, however, that doesn't necessarily date this song. The sound of it evokes more of a calliope (a steam whistle organ commonly used to evoke a fairground or circus

atmosphere) or organ sound than anything and makes a romp of a song that hops along with the listener.

Of any song on the album, you can sense the fun Linda had while recording the track. She is able to switch between simple singing (that veers closely to just talking) to her more soaring vocals that are punchy and help hammer home the message that she misses chatting with the subject of the song. While it is a quick breeze of a song, it's a fun diversion.

Ronstadt, reflecting in a 2020 interview with *Billboard*, addressed the controversy of Costello badmouthing her version of his songs:

> I understood exactly where he was coming from and why it had bothered him. If you do something and then you see someone else doing it, you think that they are taking away part of your identity. It's a sensitive reaction; I've done it myself. And I took it for what it was back then. But I love Elvis. He writes like an old-fashioned songwriter. His songs are so beautifully tragic and they have a lot of meaning behind them. He's a gentleman, and he's got a great heart.

Costello himself has acknowledged the important role Ronstadt played in keeping his career going when she first covered his song 'Alison' two years prior and now recognizes Linda's interpretations of his songs as valid and a positive thing.

Bonus Tracks

'Rambler Gambler' (traditional)

Arranged by Linda Ronstadt

This song was released as the B-side to the single release of 'How Do I Make You' and is as far from the new wave sound Ronstadt cultivated on the album as possible. Hearkening back to her country rock roots that made her a superstar in the first place, it is a slow song driven by acoustic guitar. This song hasn't ever been released beyond the single, which is a shame as Linda's vocals are as near perfection as ever on the song. This song may have been a remnant from a past recording session. Regardless of when it was recorded, it was pulled out here for the purposes of getting airplay on the country charts (it reached number 42 on the *Billboard* Country chart), where Ronstadt was still quite popular.

'The Shoop Shoop Song (It's In His Kiss)' (Clark)

Ronstadt's appearance on *The Muppet Show* took place in 1980 as well and features her singing this classic song alongside Janice and a couple of other female-presenting Muppets. The storyline of her episode is that she is in love with Kermit the Frog and the song is sung while she is clutching a picture of him. Ronstadt never recorded this song as a release, so it's our opportunity to see the fun she has with the number and what could have been. She also sang this song on an episode of *Saturday Night Live* as a duet with Phoebe Snow (in 1978) and had a similar amount of fun on-screen interpreting the song.

The Pirates Of Penzance

In what would be a career-defining moment, Linda Ronstadt stepped away from recording music shortly after *Mad Love* was released in order to star in a Central Park production of *The Pirates Of Penzance*. The 1980s would see Ronstadt utilize her voice in different ways and, more importantly, do what she wanted to do with her career. Due to her astounding success in the recording industry, Linda had the capital and luxury to explore other ways to express herself. Later in the decade, this would come in the form of recording albums unlike any of those that came before, as she released a string of American jazz standard albums, followed by one of traditional Mexican mariachi music. However, the path to those albums and, truly, the start of the rest of her career started with her experience performing in *Pirates*.

The offer to star in the production came via a phone call from show producer Joe Papp. Linda's boyfriend at the time, California Governor Jerry Brown, took the call when she was in the shower. When she emerged, he told her Papp had offered her a role in *HMS Pinafore*. Ronstadt called him back and while she was slightly disappointed it wasn't *Pinafore* (her favorite Gilbert and Sullivan operetta from childhood), she was delighted to accept the opportunity to do something different.

Ronstadt had a conversation with John Rockwell, who, by that time, was the music critic for the *New York Times*. 'I wanted to get involved in something that could utilize some of the areas of my singing that I wasn't able to utilize in the pop music field', she said:

> I wanted it to be within the context of something that I thought would be high quality, with people I thought would be high quality, so that I could learn from them. But not where I had to be the center of attraction, or where I would have to have full responsibility for the show.

Linda tackled the material head-on, rehearsing each day with the cast and then having vocal lessons in the evening. The payoff from the experience is that she was able to strengthen her voice, holding notes longer and louder than she had previously been able to. This would then propel her abilities to even greater heights and become the hallmark of her albums for the rest of the decade. Her vocals had always been powerful prior to this experience, but limits didn't really exist for her from here on in.

The performances at Central Park turned into a run of the show on Broadway. As Ronstadt said of Asher in her memoir, he was entirely supportive of this career move but was a bit hesitant that it broke up the cycle they had going of cutting an album and then touring to support it. Ronstadt taking a role in *Pirates* meant that the very lucrative music career was put on pause. Linda was right in making this move, as it gave her more experience with her voice and with stage presence. The way in which she used her body was negligible in her concerts prior to this. Afterwards, as she toured to support subsequent albums, she created more of a show for her live audiences.

The run on Broadway inspired a cast recording of the show. Linda has many great moments on the album, but 'Poor Wandering One' is her showcase and the best example of what vocal training had done for her voice. The run on Broadway was such a success that a movie was made, with Linda reprising her role as Mabel. Although far from a box office success, it's a fun video that is available to this day and is an entirely different way to see Ronstadt perform.

Get Closer (1982)

Personnel:
Linda Ronstadt: lead vocals, backing vocals
Bill Payne: Wurlitzer electric piano, acoustic piano, string arrangements and conductor, organ, Fender Rhodes, synthesizers, keyboards
Lindsey Buckingham: accordion
Don Grolnick: Prophet-5, organ
Andrew Gold: electric guitar, acoustic guitar, percussion, harmony vocals, acoustic piano
Danny Kortchmar: electric guitar
Waddy Wachtel: electric guitar, acoustic guitar
Dan Dugmore: pedal steel guitar, electric guitar
David Grisman: mandolin
Bob Glaub: bass guitar
Russ Kunkel: drums
Peter Asher: percussion
Jerry Peterson: saxophone
Jim Horn: baritone saxophone
Dennis Karmazyn: cello
Patti Austin: backing vocals
Rosemary Butler: backing vocals
Edie Lehmann: backing vocals
Debbie Pearl: backing vocals
Produced at George Massenburg Studio, Los Angeles and Record One, Los Angeles between August 1981 and August 1982 by Peter Asher (Brian Ahern produced 'My Blue Tears')
Release date: September 1982
Highest chart place: US: 31
Running time: 36:31

The creation of this album stemmed from the need for Linda Ronstadt to produce something for Asylum, as she still had one record left on her contract. Originally, according to the Rhino website, Ronstadt was going to give them a record of American Standards produced by Jerry Wexler. After recording the entire album, she decided it did not meet her high expectations and it was scrapped entirely. Although the tracks for this project, entitled *Keeping Out Of Mischief*, may still exist somewhere, it's doubtful whether Ronstadt would ever approve their release.

Ronstadt opted to return to the studio with Peter Asher to hammer out the majority of this record, as they knew they worked well together. The album is a return to the style that listeners expected of her; some of the more surprising song choices present on *Mad Love* are absent from this album. While antipathy wouldn't be the correct term for what Ronstadt may have been feeling when creating this album, it's obvious she was ready for something new, and returning to the well of what had made her successful in the past wasn't something she was very passionate about.

The result of this album's success was a reflection of that lack of passion, although it is evident Ronstadt had fun choosing these tracks and singing them. This is the first album to only achieve Gold status and the first to not reach the Top Five on the albums chart since 1973's *Don't Cry Now*, which was the album released immediately before Ronstadt made it big in pop music with *Heart Like A Wheel*. The album also has a short run time; most of the songs clock in under three minutes. Even this completed album has an unreleased track, as Ronstadt recorded a version of the Everly Brothers' 'The Price Of Love' that still hasn't been heard since it was scrapped from the album before its release.

Kosh and Ron Larson, who designed the album cover and sleeve, won the Grammy for Best Album Package. Their dynamic design included Ronstadt in a red polka dot dress (with white dots) against a white polka dot background (with red dots).

'Get Closer' (Carroll)

The opening title track is an 80s treat of electric piano pop. Written by Jon Carroll, best known as a member of the Starland Vocal Band, the song is an enticing number with the singer asking their interest to physically get closer to them. Ronstadt has a wonderful growl to her voice at points as she asks the subject to follow their heart and forget their head. Peter Asher's deft production is felt right away, as this track includes layered electric guitars from no less than three people. The background vocals contributed by Patti Austin and Rosemary Butler punctuate Linda's vocals and really heighten the pop nature of the entire track.

This song earned Linda a Grammy nomination for Best Rock Vocal Performance, Female; however, she lost out to Melissa Manchester's recording of 'You Should Hear How She Talks About You'. Stephen Holden, writing for *The New York Times*, gave high praise to Ronstadt's performance on this track, comparing her vocals to Aretha Franklin's on 'Respect' and calling it 'the album's most adventurous performance'.

The success of this song was pushed, in part, by a dynamic music video featuring Linda in the outfit seen on the award-winning album cover. She puts her Broadway acting chops to good use and is dynamic in the music video, actively moving in accordance with the lyrics. The song, released as the lead single from the album, reached number 29 on the *Billboard* Hot 100. No doubt the music video played a part in the song's popularity, as MTV was still relatively new and any song getting played on the channel translated into record sales. While this wasn't the first music video Linda made, it was the first that was produced with the MTV viewing public in mind.

Ronstadt recorded an extended version of the song that didn't make the album. It included these lyrics, which were ultimately cut from a middle verse:

Why you layin' on all that Macho stuff
Don't you think she's already had enough

'The Moon Is A Harsh Mistress' (Webb)

The tinkling piano intro leads us to a wonderful showcase of Linda's Broadway-honed voice. The sweet Jimmy Webb composition is a perfect vehicle for her new skills, as she makes this sweeping symphonic song all her own. Bill Payne, who played the electric piano on the prior track, plays the acoustic piano here. He pulled double duty, as he also arranged and conducted the strings.

Strings play a big role in this song, as they make it sound like a big production piece from a show. While strings were no stranger to Ronstadt, they really make a statement on a song like this. Their presence here serves as a preview of what her stronger voice could do when backed with a classical arrangement; this would be an important facet for the next three albums after this. This track doesn't feature any of the traditional rock instruments, which is a bold move for an album geared toward pop audiences. Its placement on the album is a good choice, as it greatly contrasts 'Get Closer', keeping the experience varied and fresh.

This is the first Jimmy Webb song on the album and the first time Linda chose to interpret one of his songs. Webb had collected Grammys all along his career and had a long association with Glen Campbell, who sang several hits penned by Webb. Webb also crafted 'Macarthur Park' for Richard Harris; this song was later recorded by Donna Summer. Both versions were hits on the charts. Jimmy and Linda performed this song together at least once; seeing the songwriter back Linda on the piano in a stripped-down, somewhat static performance showed that theatrics weren't needed in order to highlight the greatness of this song.

'I Knew You When' (South)

This track was the first cover of a rock classic on the album. Anyone listening to oldies radio was familiar with this song, as it was a staple of AM and FM station rotations. Joe South, who wrote and originally recorded the song back in 1965, had chart success with the song, as did Donny Osmond in 1971. Ronstadt's gender reversal gives the song a different edge, underscored by a decidedly 1980s rock flavor in collaboration with producer Peter Asher. From the opening line consisting of many 'yeahs', listeners would know they were in for a reinterpretation of a song with which they had passing familiarity; rather than the soft 'yeahs' heard on the original track, Ronstadt's staccato delivery pronounced the track as a harder reimagination.

Both this and the previous track gave Ronstadt an opportunity to show her voice in a way listeners may not have heard it before. The previous track was a chance to hear her in a classical setting, while Ronstadt's vocals on this track provided listeners with the way her voice could be applied to the pop genre. The last high notes, as Ronstadt pushes her voice to the stratosphere, are a wake-up call that she had grown by leaps and bounds since her prior pop album. Although only two years had passed since *Mad Love*, it was a virtual lifetime of vocal development that Ronstadt had gained in the interceding time. Between the harder choruses, Ronstadt is able to show off softer melodic singing; the swing between the rocking choruses and lulls in between gave Linda a lot of room to exercise her voice and play with the song's arrangement.

This song was released as the second single from the album, reaching number 37 on the *Billboard* Hot 100; interestingly, it also climbed to 84 on the country chart. Although Ronstadt had left behind country rock, she still had a loyal country fan base and country radio stations were still spinning her latest record. It was backed by a music video, which consisted of shooting Ronstadt and her band in a studio as if they were giving a performance. Ronstadt's camera presence had visibly improved since similar music videos were set in a studio two years prior. The increased production quality and enthusiasm for producing such a promotional film were boosted due to the medium being a proven way to generate record sales.

'Easy For You To Say' (Webb)

This track provides a cool down from 'I Knew You When', which ended rather dramatically, both vocally and instrumentally. The song, the second by Jimmy Webb on the album, is interpreted coolly by Ronstadt and almost feels like a conversation she is having with each individual listener. She keeps the tone conversational until she finds the right time to break out emotionally and vocally. Her big voice is kept under tight control throughout the track and the listener, well aware of the heights she is able to reach with that voice, can appreciate the exercise in restraint Linda exhibits. The ethereal end, with Linda cooing to lead the track to fade out, provides listeners with a soft landing. It should come as no surprise that this song reached the Top Ten on the *Billboard* Adult Contemporary chart, as its seductive magnificence makes for enjoyable listening.

'People Gonna Talk' (Wheeler/Dorsey/Levy/Lewis)

This tune kicks up the energy of the album and leads off with something that almost dates it to the time of its creation – a very infectious saxophone hook. The 1980s was the time for the saxophone to shine and this track is one of the places it is showcased to great effect by the arrangement put together by Ronstadt and Asher. At its core, this is an upbeat number that is a welcome jazzier flavor on the album; the listener can hear Linda's pleasure in her performance. It's the kind of song to get up and shake loose to.

Linda may have been drawn to this song not only for its musical structure but also the underlying message of the lyrics. The subject of tabloid rumors for over a decade, Ronstadt was a constant news item. Her private life was constantly speculated about and she was linked to many men, some she had never even met. Ronstadt shared as much on *The Tonight Show* while promoting this album, telling Johnny Carson that news items were made out of nothing simply to drive sales of magazines. This was her first appearance on the late-night staple in 14 years; she shied away from many television appearances because she preferred to just play music and hone her craft, rather than give interviews that may pry into her very private personal life.

'Talk To Me Of Mendocino' (McGarrigle)

Guest musician – Kenny Edwards: acoustic bass guitar

Linda's return to the work of one of the McGarrigle sisters (Kate, in this instance) is notable enough for this track. The song drips with longing and emotion and Linda pours everything she has into making it a believable, resonant track. Speaking to *Esquire* magazine in 1985, Ronstadt reflected on the struggle to create her interpretation: 'I didn't record it for years because I couldn't not cry trying to sing it'.

Asher's production bears mentioning, as he was directing some of the most delicate work on the album with this particular song. Considering the raucous nature (comparatively) of the previous song, this one mandated a gentle touch to make sure the lush sounds produced by the instruments had time to breathe and make a statement of their own. David Grisman, whose mandolin work was previously heard on *Prisoner In Disguise*, returns to play the same instrument prominently on this track. Andrew Gold, whose work is all over this album, plays such a gentle acoustic guitar that it blends into the overall musical landscape of the song. Fleetwood Mac's Lindsey Buckingham even came into the studio, taking on accordion duties. The result of everyone's efforts is a beautiful song that oozes sentimentality and shows the maturity of Ronstadt's development as a musical interpreter.

'I Think It's Gonna Work Out Fine' (McCoy/McKinney)

Guest musicians – James Taylor: lead and backing vocals, Rick Shlosser: drums

Ike and Tina Turner originally released this song more than two decades prior when it was a highly popular single for the duo. For the version on this album, Linda chose to duet with James Taylor, her longtime friend and, additionally, a fellow artist managed by Peter Asher. Due to their shared managerial relationship, it was easy to coordinate schedules to have studio time together. The version that the Turners recorded is much more of a call-and-response than what Ronstadt arranged. Tina Turner's vocals are much more aggressive than Linda's version, as she softened her vocals to create something more subdued that paired well with Taylor's singing style.

It's a smart pick to lead off the second side of the record, as it injects some energy into the listening experience having just heard the slow, but beautiful McGarrigle number that ended the first side of the record. The song also includes a false end, which is very rare for a Ronstadt recording. As the music cuts out, the track lingers for a couple of seconds before the beat comes back in. The real ending gives Ronstadt and Taylor a few more lines to duet on, which is a real treat when one realizes it's almost a bonus to the whole track.

'Mr. Radio' (Taylor)

If the use of saxophone didn't yet place the album solidly in the 1980s, the opening synthesizer on this track definitely would. The juxtaposition of the synthesizer with the more country rock feel of the rest of the song makes it a unique addition to the album and, perhaps, to the Ronstadt discography overall. The synthesizer comes back in the middle of the song, playing with the other instruments to make an almost surreal experience for the listener. The distortion applied to the song makes it sound futuristic and a bit mind-bending – an unusual way for Ronstadt to construct a middle eight.

Contributing to the nostalgic feel of this song, along with the country rock mood, is Andrew Gold playing a prominent part both instrumentally and vocally. The song lends itself to the blend of the old and new, with the synthesizer perhaps standing in for someone trying to tune a radio. This track really does stand alone on the album and merits a listen.

'Lies' (Randell/Charles)

Another of Ronstadt's selections from the annals of rock history, she chose this song as a vehicle to really break out her rock vocals and let loose in a manner not afforded on some of the other tracks. It also gives Linda the opportunity to apply her trained voice, used to sustain notes on the Broadway stage, to a rock track that requires some serious energy and enthusiasm to be poured into it. The version originally released by the Knickerbockers is a bit slower. Linda took the song and amped up the tempo, making a rollicking track to work her way through. It's a fast-paced interpretation of another staple of oldies radio, which makes it fresh and spunky for listeners.

This song was accompanied by a music video that was probably filmed on the same day as 'I Knew You When'. Linda fronts her band and belts out the song, making her case to the camera and singing directly to the audience. Dressed in a striped sweater with a messy, short-side ponytail for a hairstyle, Ronstadt leans into the rocker image and has fun with the song. The video is a bit more chaotic than that recorded for 'I Knew You When', so it may have been more of an afterthought to record a video for this song. They may have had more studio time with the crew and decided to go forward with it, as the video would have been solely supporting album sales by its play on MTV. As 'Lies' was not a single from the album, it didn't necessarily need a video. Despite that, it's a fun addition for those Ronstadt fans who wanted more content out of her.

'Tell Him' (Berns)

Guest musician – Rick Shlosser: drums

By selecting this song to interpret, Ronstadt really created a one-two punch on this side of the record. Another song listeners may have been familiar with from heavy play on oldies radio by this time, Linda wisely chose another upbeat song with which to have some creative fun. First made popular by The Exciters in 1962, their version featured a typical pop arrangement: strong instrumentation, catchy lyrics, and a chorus that stays with the listener long after the song has ended – the type of song someone can catch themselves humming days later. The vocals on this best-known version are strong and loud – something Linda would have been drawn to. This would also fit the mold of several songs on the records, which were oldies reinterpreted through the Ronstadt lens. Out of any of them, though, this song sticks most closely to the original.

The song is so closely tied to the previous album track that even its music videos are connected – and remain so on the official Rhino YouTube account. Linda appears the exact same and it's easy to see that she and the band rolled from one song right to the other, with a few different takes in order to get different angles of Ronstadt and her band playing. These music videos are dissimilar to those promotional films for songs from the 1970s, as everyone is obviously playing along to the recorded track and not creating a different version of the same song for the video.

Actually, there's a second music video as well. It takes place in a drive-in movie theater in the middle of winter and Ronstadt is seated in the car's passenger seat for the entire thing. There's no one in the driver's seat and Linda looks legitimately cold for the duration of the video; it does not appear to have been a fun music video shoot and seems to have taken quite a while to film, as there are noticeable natural lighting differences.

'Sometimes You Just Can't Win' (Stover)

Guest musicians – J. D. Souther: lead and harmony vocals; Rick Marotta: drums; Kenny Edwards: bass guitar

This track throws the brakes on the momentum gathered over the previous two songs as this is Ronstadt's chance to sing a ballad. This song had actually been sitting in the can for a half-decade before Linda pulled it out for inclusion on this album. This is rare; if a song was considered good enough while recording, it would typically go on the next album. Holding onto tracks and then releasing them on a different album was not something Linda or Peter Asher did during her career.

As noted in the album's liner notes, this song was originally recorded on 3 June 1977, which places it at around the time of the *Simple Dreams* sessions. The reasoning behind why this song was left off that album and resurrected for this one is unknown, especially as it was a fully finalized track that was put onto this album in the early 1980s. Due to this, it really is a journey back to the earlier part of Ronstadt's career, including her harmonizing with J. D. Souther. It is country rock at its core and provides a nice window back in time.

'My Blue Tears' (Parton)

Guest musicians – Emmylou Harris: acoustic guitar, lead and backing vocal; Dolly Parton: lead and backing vocals

This song was recorded separately from anything else on the album and, again, was recorded years prior. With its inclusion, as well as the track prior to it, you really get the sense that Ronstadt needed to fill out the album and didn't want to record any other new material. After all, the whole reason this album exists is due to Ronstadt needing to give the company one more to fulfill her contract.

If the previous track was a glimpse into Linda's past, this one afforded listeners a glimpse into her future due to the personnel singing on the album. The selection of this song was a tacit move by Ronstadt to hint at one of her desires, which was to record an entire album with pals Emmylou Harris and Dolly Parton. It was originally recorded on 18 January 1978, when the three were first trying to record an album together. Linda talked to Peter Herbst of *Rolling Stone* about the creation of this song in an interview that was printed in the 19 October 1978 issue of the magazine:

> We recorded some stuff, but let me tell you, we did it in ten days. Now, I've never made a record in less than three and a half months, and I don't think Dolly has, and I don't think Emmy has either. But we got scared because Emmy had to go on the road and Dolly had to start writing her album and I only had a certain amount of time off, and we wanted to do it so badly. I remember Dolly just making these decisions ... Well, it wouldn't have mattered if Jesus Christ and Buddha had been producing that album – you can't do something like that in ten days. We thought that somehow we would just break all the rules and we would do it, and we didn't.

While doing an album at that point proved to be impossible, the production of this song was proof enough that when the three could make the stars align, the result would be fantastic. The harmonies that the three crafted here are crushingly beautiful and channel new life into this song originally penned by Parton in 1971. It's a very sweet, languid way to end an album that showcases such a wide variety of songs and musical styles.

What's New (1983)

Personnel
Linda Ronstadt: vocals
Don Grolnick: grand piano
Tommy Tedesco: guitar
Dennis Budimir: guitar
Ray Brown: bass
Jim Hughart: bass
John Guerin: drums
Plas Johnson: tenor sax solo
Bob Cooper: tenor sax solo
Chauncey Welsch: trombone solo
Tony Terran: trumpet solo
Nelson Riddle: arrangements and conductor
Leonard Atkins: concertmaster
Nathan Ross: concertmaster
Produced at The Complex between 30 June 1982 and 4 March 1983 by Peter Asher
Release date: September 1983
Highest chart places: US: 3, UK: 31
Running time: 36:35

After a disastrous first attempt at making a standards album, a lost album that was scrapped and now only exists in bootleg form, Linda Ronstadt evaluated how else she could record the songs she loved so much. 'I never felt that rock 'n' roll defined me', Ronstadt wrote in her memoir. And why was she making this move? 'I felt I was set free to do the sounds that I'd heard growing up', Ronstadt told Jeff Kahliss of the Alta Journal, 'And it came naturally when I started studying the singers who came before me'. What she really wanted to do was work with a full orchestra and someone like Nelson Riddle, who had arranged and conducted for years and worked with some of the greats that Linda so admired. Peter Asher placed a call to Riddle and said Linda would like to meet with him. Nelson Riddle, to his credit, had no clue who Ronstadt was. He asked his daughter and the response she gave him was, 'Well, Dad, the check won't bounce'. He agreed to meet.

At the meeting, Linda asked him if he would arrange a few tracks on the upcoming album – she didn't want to presume he wanted to do everything. On the contrary, Ronstadt wrote, '...the Beatles had once asked him to write an arrangement for a track on one of their albums. He had firmly declined, saying that he didn't do tracks, only albums. I whipped out the list of songs I had chosen. "Can you do all these?" I asked. He said he could'. Thus, Linda was able to secure the arranger and composer of her dreams and set about making the album. 'I gave him general guidelines, leaving the musical intricacies of the orchestrations up to him.'

Recording this album was challenging in that Ronstadt had to adapt her usual way of recording: 'The enormous cost of working with a 40-piece orchestra meant that I wouldn't be able to rehearse with it beforehand, and we wouldn't be able to spend hours working on one song, building it a few tracks at a time the way we had recorded 'You're No Good'', Ronstadt wrote. However, Ronstadt had less of a task when it came to the actual singing:

> Rock 'n' roll diehards in the music press wondered why I had abandoned Buddy Holly for the Gershwins. The answer is that there was so much more room for me to stretch and sing. Working in *Pirates* had developed my head voice; singing standards gave me a way to marry it to my chest voice to form what voice teachers call singing in a 'mix'.

Despite trepidation from the press about this venture, Linda's instincts were correct – she could be successful at whatever she applied herself to. The album went triple platinum (factoring in international sales, the album sold over five million copies), paving the way for two more standards albums to immediately follow. It spent 81 weeks on the chart – it was still on the chart when the follow-up album, *Lush Life,* came out. The only albums blocking it from reaching number one were Michael Jackson's *Thriller* and Lionel Richie's *Can't Slow Down*. Ronstadt earned a Grammy nomination in the Best Pop Vocal Performance, Female category, showing the crossover appeal of an album filled with songs that appeared primarily in the 1920s, 1930s and 1940s. It was an incredible show of force for an album that had been doubted by everyone from Peter Asher to leadership at Asylum Records.

'What's New' (Burke/Haggart)

Linda Ronstadt's first track is a pronouncement of her mastery when it comes to American Standards. Perhaps more than any other album in her catalog, the choice of which song should go first was vitally important in setting up the probable success of the entire venture. By this time, Ronstadt was experienced enough to know what would sell and what she could do to sell the material. Her experience, combined with the consultation of Asher and collaboration with Riddle, guided her to choose this song to kick off a new era in her musical career. While it is tempting to chalk it up to fate, it's rather the opposite; it's a canny business move that would allow Ronstadt to continue to follow her musical interests and instincts.

This was the first track recorded for the album and, as it turns out, what the listener hears is the first take from the recording sessions. 'First, we ran through the arrangement for the benefit of the orchestra', Ronstadt wrote, 'We started recording, and I sang it three times. We used the first take and kept the vocal. This meant that what wound up on the record was me singing the song for the first time ever with that arrangement and in that key'.

Her prowess is on full display, sustaining long notes that create a cascade of sound that flows like a river throughout the entirety of the song. Culturally, there was no reason why this song should have been so successful; Ronstadt used her reputation and made it not only a moment in the cultural zeitgeist but made it mainstream. Although, as the lead single, it only reached 53 on the *Billboard* Hot 100, it was a force to be reckoned with on the *Billboard* Adult Contemporary chart. Although this was the first single from the album, it wasn't released until the month following the album's release. This is a contrast from her past albums, where a lead single came out before or on the same day as the entire album. The album, thus, was given the ability to stand on its own novelty prior to a single dropping from it.

Even more audacious than releasing it as a single was tapping into the music video movement and pouring resources into filming. The song's video leaned into the visuals popular at the time, as period pieces (in this case, roughly the 1940s) were seeing a resurgence, especially in popular movies such as *Indiana Jones*. It was the public's first opportunity to see Ronstadt in her full glory, hinted at on the album cover, and was her opportunity to dress the part and fully embrace the time period in the song. It also gave her a leading man to direct her singing towards, which was a first for a Ronstadt music video. Prior videos for songs from *Mad Love* and *Get Closer* were, for the most part, performance videos in which Ronstadt and her band sang to the camera. Ronstadt leveraged her acting experience to make this more cinematic in nature.

'I've Got A Crush On You' (Gershwin/Gershwin)

A selection from the Gershwins is next. Riddle keeps the orchestration low-key and supportive as Linda slinks through the performance, making it electric with sensuality as she shapes the words into her own collection of toys. Her ability to slip into a song such as this would be a hallmark of this and the following two records. Rather than seeing the performance as a cover, the way in which Ronstadt sings the song makes it feel like it's always been hers. The worn-in feeling of comfort as she glides over the notes, making them melt like butter, draws the listener in and holds their rapt attention for the runtime of the song.

Linda also made a video for this song due to it being the second single from the album. Where the video for 'What's New' felt more noir, this feels like it could have been filmed in the background of a *Thin Man* movie. The club vibe, paired with Ronstadt performing to a well-dressed audience, before dancing with a dashing suitor, makes the video seep with luxury. The viewer is invited into the fantasy and it has much the same effect as the audio track, leaving an individual wholly engrossed in Linda's performance.

'Guess I'll Hang My Tears Out To Dry' (Cahn/Styne)

The arrangement for this song places the orchestra more front and center, with it being given a healthy introduction before Ronstadt enters. The subject of this song – a sad woman lamenting a lost love – is familiar territory for longtime Linda fans. However, she was able to find a beautiful way to express this familiar feeling with a song by the duo of Jule Styne and Sammy Cahn. Since it was introduced in the 1940s, it was known as a torch song, which made it perfect for interpretation by the queen of 'torchy rock', as *Time* described her brand in a cover story in 1977. This was the first song she sang with Riddle leading up to the recording of the album. 'Nelson fished around in his briefcase and produced the original sketch of the orchestration he had done for Sinatra… He crossed out Sinatra's key and wrote in mine', Ronstadt recalled in her memoir. As work progressed on the song, 'I asked for a modulation to a higher key, to give the arrangement a lift. Nelson surprised me by showing me a way to modulate to a lower key, providing an elegant shift of mood'.

Despite the heavier orchestral arrangement, Ronstadt's vocals still shine through and she is given some great opportunities to do the heavy lifting on the track. Ronstadt's performance of this song live in Japan in 1984 shows how she became more comfortable with the material as time went on. The live version seemed even more smooth than the one laid down on vinyl and the visual of Linda in front of a darkened orchestra, singing on a huge stage for a rapt audience, emphasizes her immense power.

'Crazy He Calls Me' (Sigman/Russell)

A sultry number that was made most famous by Billie Holiday, Ronstadt tackles this standard with the same energy and vigor that she applied to the prior tracks on the album. Plas Johnson, who would contribute saxophone to all three standards albums, makes his first appearance on this track, and the use of his alto sax skills, especially in the solo, help accentuate the mood of the song and the words expressed by Linda. An understated number with spare orchestration, it served as one of the signature switch-ups on a Ronstadt album; typically seen in a switch between genres on her previous albums, she and Asher worked on making sure similarly orchestrated songs were not paired up on the album. Although this album has, arguably, songs from the same genre, Linda's song choices and the way in which they were presented on the album ensured listeners wouldn't get bored while listening.

'Someone To Watch Over Me' (Gershwin/Gershwin)

For the second time on the album, Linda turned to the Gershwins for a composition. It originally started off as a more playful number, as intended by George Gershwin, but in subsequent years, after it was introduced in 1926, it transformed into a slower jazz piece. Riddle had previously done an arrangement of this song in 1959 for Keely Smith, so he was familiar with how it could be changed based on who was singing the tune. There are close to 2,000 recordings of this song in existence; however, Linda's version of the song may be one of the measuring sticks to which others are compared due to her strong vocals and the subtle string arrangement backing her. This was the third and last single from the album, released in the spring of 1984 to keep the momentum for the album going. Her next album, *Lush Life,* would arrive before the end of the year.

In a concert video produced for the album, Ronstadt fans could watch her run through many of the numbers on the album. Regarding this song, an interesting aspect of the video is the emphasis on the flautist, who lends an air of innocence and a touch of whimsiness to the interpretation. In an arrangement such as this, it can be easy to overlook certain instruments because the track itself is lush and flooded with wonderful sounds. By seeing it performed live, listeners were able to garner a better understanding of the track's instrumentation.

'I Don't Stand A Ghost Of A Chance With You' (Crosby/Washington/Young)

Bob Cooper takes over saxophone duties here, drawing the listener in and leading them towards Ronstadt's vocal performance. Aside from the saxophone, the orchestration on this track is sparse, allowing Linda's vocals to stand alone. Another song that gives her ample room to showcase the mastery of her voice, Ronstadt's performance on this track is beautiful and elegant, understated and subtle. It's the type of song that listeners could luxuriate in, with no pressure to seek a deeper lyrical meaning. From such a standpoint, it's a straightforward song to understand and appreciate – the singer of the song knows that she doesn't have a chance with the guy she's pining for. The combination of all these factors makes it an unmissable song on the album.

A music video was filmed for this song, but its visual representation followed the audio cues closely. Compared to the previous two videos produced for the album, there is no real theatricality. Instead, much like the audio track, the two main focuses are on Linda's singing and the saxophone performance. It made its statement with the music, rather than any hallmark of early music videos, and pairs quite well with the song.

'What'll I Do' (Berlin)

Ronstadt's exploration of material by Irving Berlin begins with this track, originally written in 1923. By the time Ronstadt released it, it had been in the cultural zeitgeist for six decades. Prior to Linda interpreting it for herself, contemporary audiences had been treated to versions by Nancy Sinatra, Harry Nilsson and Cher in the previous decade and a half.

Ronstadt's version is given the full orchestral arrangement, and paired with her outstanding vocals, she makes a memorable entry into this song's history. The challenging part of singing any of these songs, as Ronstadt knew coming into such a project, is that you have to do something distinctive. Her choice of Riddle as her conductor made all the difference and forced the recent versions to fade into history, as his mastery of the orchestra and ability to arrange brought out the best in the musicians he stood in front of. The longing vocals Linda applies to Riddle's arrangement pull at the heartstrings, imploring the listener to invest in the story of forlorn love and the heartbreaking separation between lovers.

'Lover Man (Oh Where Can You Be?)' (Davis/Sherman/Ramirez)
This track can almost be considered a duet with Chauncey Welsch and his trombone. Another classic that may be best known as a Billie Holiday song, Linda took it on and applied some very sweet vocals to emphasize her search for the perfect man. Again, Ronstadt's vocal training is audibly present as she smooths one note into another, providing a silky embrace as the record spins on the turntable. On the home video release of her concert with Nelson Riddle, Linda appears as a taffeta dream, floating in to deliver the equally dreamy vocals. Ronstadt obviously enjoyed the opportunity to dress in period costume, as it set not only the mood for what concertgoers could expect but also paid tribute to the greats before her.

'Goodbye' (Jenkins)
This song was known as the one with which the Benny Goodman orchestra ended their sets, so it's fitting that Linda chose it as the closing track. Benny Goodman was still alive at the time of this record's release, so it's to be hoped that he appreciated the inclusion of this song on Ronstadt's record, especially with such a deft arrangement by Nelson Riddle. This territory was well-known to Riddle, who had previously arranged the song for both Frank Sinatra and Ella Fitzgerald. In other words, Ronstadt was in very good hands. Her vocals here are next level, beginning slow and mournful before powering up to her strongest level.

This track, more than any other, feels cinematic in nature. The drama Riddle injected into the arrangement is a wonderful playground for any vocalist to have at their disposal, but it spoke to not only Linda's instincts as a singer but also as an all-around performer. It's natural, then, that a music video was produced to capitalize on the sound of this track. The same club set was used for the videos connected to this album, but each song made it feel like a different setting. The video begins on the street and then goes into the club where Linda is performing; after the first verse, Ronstadt leaves the stage and the club, walking into the alley where the action started. Ronstadt's character paints a lonely portrait of her life as the viewer leaves her alone, after the last note, on the street.

Bonus Track
'Real Emotional Girl' (Newman)
Despite being deep into the American Songbook phase of her career, Linda guested on the HBO special 'Randy Newman: At The Odeon' in December

1983. In her only known performance of this song, Ronstadt took the words and music from Newman and incorporated her own flair. It's a rare pop music performance by Ronstadt during this time. It's easy to imagine that Linda would have chosen this song for an album had she continued producing pop albums. Instead, this is a rarity that must be sought out to be experienced. It's a quiet and simple performance, accompanied only by Newman on the piano, but it is powerful in its own right.

Lush Life (1984)

Personnel:
Linda Ronstadt: vocals
Nelson Riddle: arrangements and conductor
Don Grolnick: grand piano, piano solo
Bob Mann: guitar
Bob Magnusson: bass
John Guerin: drums
David Frisina: concertmaster, violin
Tommy Morgan: harmonica
Tony Terran: trumpet solo
Plas Johnson: tenor sax solo
Louis Bellson: drums
Oscar Brashear: trumpet solo
Chauncey Welsh: trombone solo
Produced at The Complex between 24 August and 5 October 1984 by Peter Asher
Release date: November 1984
Highest chart places: US: 13, UK: 100
Running time: 41:29

Despite skepticism about the possible success of *What's New*, the combination of Linda Ronstadt and Nelson Riddle proved irresistible to the record-buying public. The winning formula demonstrated to them both that they were onto something big, which caused them to immediately begin planning for this album. The Great American Songbook has many songs contained within it, so having material for a second album wasn't an issue at all. Ronstadt and Riddle picked out another album full of classics that might have been familiar, one way or another, to listeners; once again, the arrangements would differ from prior versions, allowing Ronstadt to have her own take with each track. This album reached platinum status very quickly – in just a few weeks – showing that the public still had a strong desire for this content. It was also Ronstadt's tenth platinum album.

The album was recognized in several ways. The album art itself, designed by longtime Ronstadt collaborator Kosh, won the Grammy Award for Best Album Package. This may be due to the die-cut design that allowed the listener to open up the hatbox, in a fashion, in order to extract the vinyl album from the package. As Kosh remembered in an interview for albumcoverhalloffame.com:

> *Lush Life* was going to be her second collaboration with Nelson Riddle & His Orchestra, and, since Linda was immersed in the big band period and the fashion of the era, I told her that I was going to put her in a hat box. I then worked with photographer Robert Blakeman and my associate Ron Larson to

develop the overall concept. I heard all of the final and rough mixes of the album as we were working on expanding our approach to the design.

Linda was nominated for the Grammy Award for Best Female Pop Vocal Performance at the 1986 awards, where she and Tina Turner, Pat Benatar and Madonna lost to Whitney Houston. Although it was primarily a jazz album, reaching number three on the Jazz Album chart, it also reached number 13 on the *Billboard* chart.

'When I Fall In Love' (Heyman/Young)

The opening track on Linda Ronstadt's second album of standards doesn't contain the full orchestral experience until a minute into the track. Instead, Ronstadt is accompanied only by a guitar as she begins this song about someone finally finding the love of their life. In contrast to the album's title, this sparse beginning cannot be described as lush. The unconventionally acoustic way in which this song is recorded is contrary to the word 'lush', as it applies to the orchestral nature of the rest of the album.

Prior to Ronstadt's recording of this song, the best-known versions may have been Doris Day's version from 1952 and Nat King Cole's from 1957. The other recording of this song that may be as well-known is Natalie Cole's duet with her father, which was released more than ten years after *Lush Life* hit the stores. Thus, Ronstadt's recording falls victim to the same issue that her rendition of 'I Will Always Love You' did: it happens to be sandwiched, historically, between two other loved versions of the same song. However, within its time, it was popular enough to rise to number 24 on the *Billboard* Adult Contemporary chart – this song was the second and final single released for the album. Ronstadt's version differs from others in the popular consciousness due to its pared-down arrangement. This shows not only Ronstadt's familiarity with the material as it existed before, but how she wanted to steer her version to a different vision of the song as a whole.

'Skylark' (Carmichael/Mercer)

The most notable instrument here is the harmonica, which is used to great effect to punctuate Linda's vocals. It brings a sense of longing to the track and perfectly complements the words as expressed by Ronstadt throughout. Harmonica is something a listener would have expected from Linda's country rock days, but its use here, outside of a country-rock context, makes it more meaningful and the track stands out more than any other early track featuring harmonica as a result.

This song, which began its life as a melody, took songwriter Johnny Mercer a year to come up with the right lyrics. What you hear Ronstadt sing are words Mercer wrote about his romance with Judy Garland. The song was an immediate hit in 1942, recorded in successful iterations by Bing Crosby, Dinah Shore and Glenn Miller and his Orchestra that year. By the time Ronstadt recorded her version, the song was well known and its previous recordings were especially familiar to those who grew up in the 1940s. In contrast to these recordings, Ronstadt and Riddle toned down the orchestration in the background and stripped away the prominent horn parts that were present four decades earlier. To accompany the deft application of the harmonica, strings were added to fill out the space.

This song was the lead single from the album and was accompanied by a music video, which sees Ronstadt preparing for a trip with her dog. The footage of Linda in vintage clothes is interspersed with her singing directly into the camera, ghosted by video footage of the harmonica player punctuating his part to evoke the solitary qualities of the song. The back cover of the album features images of Ronstadt and two dogs, with an airplane in the background, which are obviously reference points for the music video.

'It Never Entered My Mind' (Hart/Rodgers)

Linda's first show tune on the album, this originally appeared in the Rodgers and Hart musical *Higher And Higher* in 1940. Frank Sinatra, Nelson Riddle's frequent collaborator, recorded this song three times before Linda had her chance with it. Riddle was familiar with this song, having arranged it for Sinatra himself on at least one occasion. The arrangement on this album strayed away from the one that may be most familiar to some listeners, which is Miles Davis' version. Davis' rendition of the track includes heavy horn and piano parts, which are absent on the Ronstadt track.

With Ronstadt's version, listeners are treated to a full orchestral introduction before she picks up her vocal duties. Linda allows herself to be carried along by the wonderful instrumentation until about the two-minute mark, at which point she exerts control with her strong emphasis on the lyrics. This song presents the listener with the most audibly identified connection to the previous album, as it is arranged and orchestrated like that whole previous album, and it was canny of Ronstadt to withhold this track until the middle of the first side of the album. It's notable that the first two tracks of the album, which also served as the two singles, were departures from the typical sound of her previous offering. With 'It Never Entered My Mind', Ronstadt was able to return to the form that worked so well with *What's New*. It wasn't necessarily new territory, but it provided her with a comfortable setting to exercise her standards singing voice and show the listener that there are still familiar places on *Lush Life* where they may seek comfort.

'Mean To Me' (Ahlert/Turk)

The origins of this song stretch back to 1929 and was recorded previously by a who's who of 20th-century singers, including Frank Sinatra, Billie Holiday, the Andrews Sisters, Judy Garland, Rosemary Clooney and Ella Fitzgerald. The protagonist of the song is chiding her love interest for being mean to them – hence the name. However, the meaning of that phrase changes throughout the course of the song, with Linda eventually singing to her lover about how much he means to her. Thus, two definitions of the word 'mean' are played within the song, giving the turn of phrase a double meaning.

This track is smooth in both instrumentation and vocals. Again, Ronstadt worked with Riddle to strip this song down to its bones and build it back up. Previous versions of the song were heavy on horns, while Riddle and Ronstadt relied more on strings to evoke emotion. Following Ronstadt's release of this song, it would be more than ten years before someone else released a recording of it; that person was Rosemary Clooney, who had already recorded it twice. In a way, Linda set a very high bar for how this song should sound and others may not have felt the need to return to it.

'When Your Lover Has Gone' (Swan)

The cadence of this song is subtle and relaxing, truly living up to the title of the album itself. Soft strings insulate the listener and Ronstadt's vocals warm them up. By the time Ronstadt had recorded this song, it had long since been a jazz standard, making its debut in 1931 alongside the James Cagney film *Blonde Crazy*. The song's writer, Einar Aaron Swan, had died tragically young at the age of 37. Among the many luminaries in the music business who sang this song was Frank Sinatra, who donated the profits from his release of the song to Swan's widow.

Plas Johnson has his first tenor saxophone solo of the album here and it is used to great effect to accent the smooth sound coaxed out of the rest of the orchestra by Riddle. Ronstadt's vocals are restrained to create the mellow tone throughout and it is, by any account, a safe pick for the middle of the album. A track like this wouldn't have been considered single-worthy at any point in the creation of the album, but it is a way for Ronstadt and Riddle to showcase a light touch on a jazz standard that could have been interpreted in a much heavier manner.

'I'm A Fool To Want You' (Herron/Sinatra/Wolf)

The orchestration and vocals here are akin to Linda Ronstadt's version of a Bond theme. Riddle channeled a good deal of John Barry when developing the arrangement for this track, which has a highly dramatic flair and contrasts nicely with the previous song. This is the only instance on this album where a song was partially created, and not just sung at some point in history, by Frank Sinatra.

Linda does an outstanding job of blasting these lyrics into the stratosphere with her amazing vocal range. She correctly translates the melancholy lyrics written by Sinatra and does an admirable job marrying the mood set by the orchestra with her longing vocal interpretation. The scope of the song is truly cinematic in nature, and by going big, it achieves a lot for everyone involved.

Whereas the prior track was subdued and quiet, this one blasts the listener out of their chair by the final closing notes of the lonely-sounding horn section, followed by the sparse tones of a limited string section.

The material in the song is familiar territory for Ronstadt, as the subject matter is similar to the songs she selected for her pop albums in the 1970s and early 1980s. To hear her lend her voice to the same type of lyrics as those that rocketed her to the top of the charts, but in an entirely different way, is a treat for those listening.

'You Took Advantage Of Me' (Hart/Rodgers)

The second song from a musical, this is also the second track on the album written by the duo of Rodgers and Hart. The history of the song stretches back to 1928 and had been familiar territory for not only music fans but also movie fans. Judy Garland sang this song during a sequence in *A Star Is Born*. Just as Garland had fun with the number in that movie, it's evident Ronstadt had fun making this her own. It's an upbeat number for Linda Ronstadt to shake loose and similarly give the listener a chance to have a little fun after a pretty heavy previous track. It features another prominent tenor saxophone solo provided by Plas Johnson. This is an appropriate number to open up the second side of the record; where 'I'm A Fool To Want You' felt like a dramatic ending, this track is a light, frothy, fun and jumpy number to provide relief and gear the listener up for the entire second half of the album.

This is a deft choice that highlights how important track order was in an environment where folks would put a record on and listen to it the whole way through. It's here, more than anyplace else on the entire record, where producer Peter Asher's experience shines through. Whereas there were subtle clues to his influence in the track order on the first side, you can see how he worked with Ronstadt to develop the journey a listener would go on by having this be the song to open up side two.

'Sophisticated Lady' (Ellington/Mills/Parish)

Duke Ellington is such a prominent name in jazz that it was a necessity for Linda to record a song written by him to feature on an album full of jazz standards. For her first song by Ellington, Ronstadt chose one where he composed the music, but the words were constructed by Irving Mills and Mitchell Parish. The lyrics of the song evoke a very svelte, elegant woman whom the singer ultimately sees as someone who is yearning for something more than the vapid trappings of material culture. While Madonna was producing 'Material Girl' around the same time, Linda was tackling similar subject matter with a more storied set of lyrics and arrangement. The similarity between the subjects of both songs can be striking if analyzed, with the subject of Madonna's song being from the woman's point of view, while Ronstadt views that woman from the outside – and maybe a few years after her heyday.

Linda's tumbling vocals follow (or direct?) the orchestra narrating the story of the titular lady. Ronstadt's vocal training from Broadway is on full view here, as her style varies from speak-singing short lines to absolutely soaring, powerful vocals at the apex of the song. Johnson uses his last saxophone solo on the album to great effect, as it bridges the narrative of the song and allows it to breathe.

'Can't We Be Friends' (James/Swift)
This Broadway tune was familiar territory for Nelson Riddle, who had previously arranged it for Frank Sinatra. This is also one of the standards on the album that has been recorded least, giving Ronstadt's version a prominent place when reviewing those that came before and after her. In fact, this song wasn't recorded again until almost 20 years after the release of this album. It may also have been familiar to listeners due to its use in several movies, including *Flamingo Road* and an instrumental version played in the background of a scene in *Bonnie & Clyde.*

An upbeat jazz number, the band are given time to establish the tempo of the song before Ronstadt enters. Another bouncy track, you can tell that Linda is having fun with this song selection. Similar to 'You Took Advantage Of Me', this song originated in the late 1920s and is a true product of the Jazz Age. It's also one of the quickest numbers on the album, clocking in at just over two minutes and 30 seconds. It's a quick break that the listener is granted, as jazz standards can sometimes be longer and more involved than this song. It's a good selection for the middle of the second side of the album.

'My Old Flame' (Coslow/Johnston)
Mae West originally sang this song in the film *Belle Of The Nineties* in 1934, after which it became a jazz standard. This is due to Duke Ellington realizing its potential and laying down a recording of it with West soon after the movie was released. By the time Ronstadt released this album, West had sort of become a parody of herself, playing up to that fact in 1978's *Sextette*. While Linda successfully strips away any of the campiness associated with West, the lyrics are playful, and discerning listeners can ascertain how the song could have begun its life as a Mae West number.

While the lyrics are longing in nature, it's comedic at the same time because the protagonist doesn't even remember the name of her old flame. Chauncey Welsh is given ample room for a subdued, but effective trombone solo. While West may have established the song, she was not as strong a vocalist as Ronstadt. Riddle's arrangement also excluded the oboe, which was very present throughout West's version.

This is an example of another song that is a buried treasure – it may not have been a single or even one of the better-known songs on the album, but Ronstadt revived it for a new generation.

'Falling In Love Again' (Hollaender/Lerner)
The beginning of this song is reminiscent of a music box, starting off very sweetly with a simple tinkling of piano keys. The beginning of the song afforded Ronstadt the chance to sing a sweet melody that, around the one-minute mark, morphs into a much jazzier number. Like the track immediately preceding it, it also originated as a song in a movie; this time, by way of Marlene Dietrich in the 1930 German language film *The Blue Angel*.

Unlike most songs on the album, this one was in the popular zeitgeist immediately preceding Ronstadt's recording of it. Harkening back to her experience drawing upon popular music for inspiration, The Beatles had made an arrangement of the song during their residency at the Cavern Club in Liverpool. Paul McCartney took lead vocals on their version, which was a simple early-Beatles track prior to their big break on the popular music scene. Peter Asher may have been aware of this version due to his closeness with the band. The more immediate release was from British singer-songwriter Kevin Ayers, whose version included heavy use of an organ against the backdrop of his deep voice.

Ronstadt and Riddle stripped the song down, giving it a more traditional jazz arrangement. Overall, it was a way for Ronstadt to showcase her Broadway-trained voice to sing sweetly; despite the transition of the song midway through, she maintains her characteristic phrasing. While not an overwhelming overhaul of a song, a listener may appreciate the straightforward nature of the track and Ronstadt's interpretation of it.

'Lush Life' (Strayhorn)
At the end of the album is where you'll find the title track. It starts with dramatic piano that quickly retreats to a simpler method of playing prior to Ronstadt beginning her vocals. The song was written over the course of three years by Billy Strayhorn and tells of someone who is tired of living the jazz lifestyle. The time signature changes during the course of the song, but Ronstadt does a wonderful job at matching her vocals with the orchestra, as conducted by Nelson Riddle. As the track speaks of weariness and loneliness, it's appropriate that it closes out the album. After all, the album gives listeners a wide selection of jazz standards.

This song was recognized by the Recording Academy, earning Nelson Riddle his third and final Grammy (sadly, after he had passed away). By winning the award for Best Instrumental Arrangement Accompanying Vocalist(s)/ Best Background Arrangement, Riddle showed that he still was able to collaborate effectively with an artist to bring instrumentation to the forefront. It's appropriate that Riddle won for his efforts on this song, as the complicated arrangement required the knowledge and experience of a master to pull it off. While each track on the album varied greatly from one to another, the variations within this one song are worth a listen. The strong collaboration between Linda and Nelson made this an effective end to their second album together.

For Sentimental Reasons (1986)

Personnel:
Linda Ronstadt: vocals
Don Grolnick: grand piano
Bob Mann: guitar
Bob Magnusson: bass
John Guerin: drums
Plas Johnson: tenor saxophone
Bud Shank: alto saxophone
Chauncey Welsch: trombone
Warren Luening: trumpet
James SK Wãn: bamboo flute
Nelson Riddle: all arrangements, conductor
Produced at The Complex between 10 July 1985 and 16 May 1986 by Peter Asher
Release date: October 1986
Highest chart place: US: 46
Running time: 42:10

Linda Ronstadt and Nelson Riddle came together one last time for this album, which proved that the interest in Ronstadt's interpretations of songs from the Great American Songbook was still sufficiently high to reward Ronstadt with her 11th platinum album. Although this was released in the fall of 1986, these three albums were so consistently popular that Asylum released a compilation of all three in the same year.

As Ronstadt explained in her musical memoir *Simple Dreams*, there were signs that Riddle was not well in the course of this album's recording. 'We discovered that he was going outside to lie down in his car during the breaks', she remembered. Despite suffering from liver disease, Riddle arranged all the songs and conducted the orchestra for all but three of the tracks on this album. 'We did the final recordings without him', Ronstadt continued, 'Some of the musicians were in tears, including his son Christopher, who played trombone in the horn section'. It was a tragic end to a musical partnership that proved a winning and lucrative combination that accomplished Ronstadt's goals of getting this sort of music out of the elevator and back into the popular zeitgeist. 'These songs are brilliantly crafted. The 1940s were absolutely the Golden Age of the popular song', Ronstadt told *USA Weekend* in November 1986, 'Today, we're in the Golden Age of record making in terms of technical production. But back then, it was songwriting at its best'.

It's tantalizing to play the game of 'what if' regarding Ronstadt's career should Riddle have lived to continue their partnership. Although she would grow from this point and explore other areas of music, she ultimately went back to popular contemporary music for the tail end of her career. While she may not have stuck to only standards albums, it's easy to imagine a world where she and Riddle would return to the studio every couple of years to produce another album in between her other endeavors. The only thing that ultimately brought this chapter of her career to a close was the loss of Nelson Riddle.

'When You Wish Upon A Star' (Harline/Washington)
This song is almost instantly recognizable as a Disney tune; in fact, it was the first Disney song to win an Academy Award. After its initial inclusion in *Pinocchio*, it was covered several times in the wake of the movie. It has become one of the trademark tunes for the Disney Company and is used, in modern times, in several contexts. One of the more prominent places is the opening credits to many Disney films, which includes an orchestral version of the song behind the visuals of the company's branding: a castle with fireworks in the background. Thus, many listeners are aware of the melody, if not the recorded version originally sung by a cartoon cricket.

By the time Linda chose this song for inclusion on her last album based on the Great American Songbook, it was already a jazz standard. In addition to being covered by a wide variety of artists associated with that genre, Gene Simmons from Kiss even recorded a version for his 1978 solo album. While Ronstadt probably didn't think of her song competing with that particular version in the minds of most people, she put forth a solid effort. After a flute introduction, she gently leads the listener into the song. The beginning transitions to Ronstadt's voice being accompanied by the piano. The track continues to build in a subtle manner, with a soft drum beat joining the piano before strings smoothly usher in the second verse. Eventually, by the end of the song, Linda is able to unleash her high notes to underscore the sweet interpretation she made of this classic.

This song was the lead single from the album and received the music video treatment. The video has a dreamy quality and features a prominent part for a ballet dancer. At the end of the video, she gives a smooch to an animated Jiminy Cricket, who blushes at the attention. It's a fun little bit of magic lent to a familiar song for generations of listeners.

'Bewitched, Bothered And Bewildered' (Hart/Rodgers)
The first of three Hart and Rodgers songs pulled from their musicals included on this album, this song was originally included in their production of *Pal Joey* in 1940. A slow shuffle of a song, it begins with a simple piano part to lead into Ronstadt's vocals. Much like the previous song, the beginning of the song is stripped down and is only joined by a drum during the first chorus. The full orchestra plays a similarly understated role in this track, which is contrary to the lush nature of the previous album. The strings and woodwinds are both toned down in this interpretation of the song, giving Linda's voice prominence over everything else on the track.

Ronstadt's affection for this song is evident as, near the end of her singing career, she chose this song as part of her set in 2006. Her voice sounds almost exactly the same as the original version – in some parts, it sounds almost stronger. It was rare for Ronstadt to hang onto songs for decades as part of her repertoire (outside of command performances where she needed to bust out one of her most recognizable pop hits). Her inclusion of this song two decades later shows that it held a special place in her heart. Listeners should start by enjoying the album version of this song, then seeking out the live version from 2006 and relishing the last note that tops the recorded version.

'You Go To My Head' (Coots/Gillespie)

Much like the champagne bubbles Ronstadt sings about, this song easily goes to the listener's head. Much like the previous songs on the album, this is very soft and stripped down. While she had been hitting some high or hard notes, overall, this song continued the mellow theme that the album was striving for.

The track opens with guitar accompaniment to Linda's vocals before being fleshed out by horns and percussion at the midway point. There is even a guitar solo in the song, which is a bit unexpected; almost as unexpected as the trumpet solo immediately afterwards. Ronstadt's interpretation doesn't focus on vocal acrobatics, but rather on enunciation and eliciting a soothing feeling of comfort. The delivery is as smooth as silk and it's easy to follow the melody and the story for the duration of the track. While it is special in its own regard, it is not as memorable as the previous two songs and fits in with what someone may expect three songs into a third album of standards from Ronstadt.

'But Not For Me' (Gershwin/Gershwin)

The Gershwins wrote this song in 1930 for *Girl Crazy*, in which Ethel Merman made her stage debut, and it became very popular as a result of that musical. This is the lengthiest song on the album and gives ample room for Ronstadt to explore its roomy corners. A shortened version of the song appeared in the film of the same name, sung by star Judy Garland.

Listeners may have been familiar with the 1959 version by Ella Fitzgerald that eventually won her the 1960 Grammy for Best Female Vocal Performance. Thus, Linda's version, released over two decades later, serves to remind listeners of the lush way in which this song could transport them to another, more relaxing place.

Riddle's expertise at conducting the orchestra can especially be felt here, as the instruments only take a front-and-center focus away from Ronstadt when she allows them to. A prime example is the saxophone solo, which evokes the same sort of feeling with its notes that Linda does; she is the trendsetter and the orchestra follows. Ronstadt's version isn't as sad as it could have been, considering the lyrics about love being impossible to find. The lyrics enumerate just how many tropes of love are not for the narrator, including lucky stars and songs written professing love for her. Instead, it presents as a sort of airy contemplation rather than a foundational piece of introspection. The way in which the song was arranged is very conducive to how the album has developed to this point.

'My Funny Valentine' (Hart/Rodgers)
Guest musicians – The Sequoia String Quartet
A jaunty string arrangement leads the listener into the track. Ronstadt's enunciation and diction are on full display in the first verse before she starts shaping her vocal with lush bends that beckon the listener to pay full attention. The playful lyrics, as Linda runs through the defects of her love interest, are made beautiful by sensitive string accompaniment. This is made more apparent on a later live performance, as Ronstadt showed she didn't need a full orchestra to pull off a stunning performance. Her voice and string quartet are able to provide an experience that may have required a full orchestra for a different caliber of performer.

The tone of the song is mournful in arrangement, with very sparse piano backing Ronstadt's downcast lyrics disparaging the subject of the song. The strings sound quite tragic, creating an overall melancholy. As it is in other versions, Linda makes her version memorable with her vocals by working with the somewhat cruel lyrics and crafting them into something more heartfelt. Being apart from the pack with this song is difficult, as it is one of the most covered songs on this album, but Ronstadt tackles it with vigor and adds her touch.

'I Get Along Without You Very Well' (Carmichael/Thompson)
This standard is one that has been covered many times since Ronstadt released this album. So why does it seem to draw not only modern listeners but also modern artists? After all, if there wasn't something special about the song, then it wouldn't still pop up in music, from artists as different as Molly Ringwald and Kristin Chenoweth choosing to tackle it. The song resonates with many listeners due to the theme of love and how an individual's lover ultimately completes them. It's an undemanding song to perform for those who choose to sing it, and the arrangement can be as complicated or as easy as a producer or artist makes it.

Ronstadt and Riddle combine forces to produce a memorable version of this song, with Riddle's deft work as a conductor and arranger evident as the orchestra develops a dreamlike aura behind Ronstadt's gorgeous vocals. The entire production of this song also owes a lot to Peter Asher for taking the raw material and turning it into a beautiful rendition of a well-trodden song from the jazz standard landscape. If Ronstadt's version isn't a benchmark for those who have since recorded it, it needs to be.

'Am I Blue?' (Akst/Clarke)

Guest musicians – Terry Woodson: conductor, Dennis Budimir: guitar, Ray Brown: bass, Louie Bellson: drums

Although all of the songs on this album can be defined as jazz, this one is more so than any other and more upbeat than most. This is the first song conducted by Terry Woodson on the album following Nelson Riddle's untimely death. Despite the conductor change, this song (like all others on the album) was arranged by Riddle, thus listeners can still hear his touch on the track.

Ronstadt is audibly having fun here; there's a bouncy, fresh quality to this song that has been missing from the entire album. While the previous tracks bring to mind a smoky lounge with Ronstadt singing to an audience sipping martinis, this song has a splashy quality that feels energetic and spunky.

This song was included in many television episodes and movies. Cher also released it as a single from her own album of standards, *Bittersweet White Light*, in 1973. The touch that Ronstadt and Riddle put on the song freshened it up from a slow jazz number to one that is a breeze of a song.

'(I Love You) For Sentimental Reasons' (Best/Watson)

Guest musicians – Terry Woodson: conductor; Mic Bell, Drake Frye, Clifford Holland, Carl Jones: backing vocals

James Brown released this song in 1976 ... as a disco single. After you allow that to sink in, don't let Brown's version be your only experience with the song. Instead, seek out this track from Ronstadt's last album of standards. In many ways, it represents her send-off to the genre by choosing it as the title track – she loved recording these songs for sentimental reasons and was a champion of the genre when most others ignored it entirely. It presents a rarity across Linda's trilogy of standards albums, as she is backed by a vocal trio for the entirety of the song. While her other work is flush with an assortment of backing or harmonizing vocalists, the inclusion of the trio comes as a bit of a pleasant surprise. The backing vocals are understated, especially when a listener indulges in other versions of this song, starting back with its release in 1946 by the King Cole Trio.

The entire production of the song makes it feel as if it is from the 'golden era' of the American songbook 30 years prior – it could easily be included on one of those albums. This is an astounding feat, as Ronstadt's interpretations usually sound fresh and new. The song is a treat for those listening to the entire album and shouldn't be skipped, as it continues the precedent set by the last song of sounding different from the first half of the album. Although Riddle was absent from conducting this number, his forethought for the arrangement bore fruit even after he was gone.

Okay, after you've enjoyed Ronstadt's version, go out and listen to Brown's version and appreciate the juxtaposition. Linda's version was the second single released for the album, coming out over six months after the album was originally released.

'Straighten Up And Fly Right' (Cole/Mills)

Guest musicians – Terry Woodson: conductor, Dennis Budimir: guitar, Ray Brown: bass, Louie Bellson: drums, James Taylor: backing vocals

The original version of this track was the biggest success for the King Cole Trio and was penned by Nat King Cole and Irving Mills. Charting in 1943, it was an established song long before Ronstadt chose it for inclusion on this album. However, much like 'I Get Along Without You Very Well', it gained more traction for artists to interpret after Ronstadt had her turn with it here.

Another upbeat song, this track continues the momentum established by the prior tracks. It's a jaunt with Ronstadt and James Taylor, providing backing vocals, along for the ride. It's a fun number and showcases some good piano-driven jazz to represent that corner of the genre. There is ample space for horns on the track, which is a bit of a surprise because this journey is a quick one. Clocking in at just over two minutes, this song is the shortest one on the album and the only one to come in under three minutes. For such a short song, it packs in a lot of joy and musicality.

'Little Girl Blue' (Hart/Rodgers)

Ronstadt returned one last time to Rodgers and Hart for this penultimate number on the album, which originally appeared in the musical *Jumbo*. True to the color in its name, the track evokes a 'blue' feeling. Both this song and the following were conducted by Riddle; this is a nice touch by Ronstadt and Asher, who put the numbers conducted by Terry Woodson between Riddle-led numbers. Whether this was conscious or not, this track sounds very similar to the others conducted by Riddle in that it has a slower tempo and is more downbeat than those conducted by Woodson.

This song may have been recorded before those that Nelson Riddle didn't have a chance to conduct due to its similar nature. This stylistic choice wouldn't have been unusual, as you can focus on getting the mood and tempo right for similar songs before moving on to those that are dissimilar, such as those that Woodson eventually conducted.

The lush orchestration amidst the soaring, liquid notes sung by Ronstadt languishes together on a lavish track that really sums up her mastery over the material she had devoted the past few years to interpreting and performing.

''Round Midnight' (Monk/Hanighen/Williams)

This song, which also lent its name to a triple album re-release of these three standards albums, closes out the album and the era of Linda interpreting classics from the Great American Songbook. The song is easily the most dramatic sounding on the album, seeming more cinematic than any other included in the assortment. Linda's vocals lean into the orchestration, and together, they paint a picture of a woman wistfully dwelling on her relationship. It's easy to see the draw of this song for Ronstadt due to both its subject material and arrangement possibilities.

It is one of the truest jazz standards chosen by Ronstadt, as it was originally written by jazz artist Thelonious Monk in the 1940s. This song is separated from many of the selections Ronstadt made for these three albums, with most of them originating as songs from musicals, etc., before finding themselves included as standards within the jazz community.

Trio (1987)

Personnel:
Linda Ronstadt: lead and harmony vocals
Emmylou Harris: lead and harmony vocals, acoustic guitar, arrangements
Dolly Parton: lead and harmony vocals
Bill Payne: acoustic piano, electric piano, Hammond organ, harmonium
Albert Lee: acoustic guitar solo, acoustic guitar, high-strung guitar, mandolin, lead acoustic guitar
Steve Fishell: pedal steel guitar, Dobro, Kona Hawaiian guitar
David Lindley: mandolin, Kona Hawaiian guitar, autoharp, harpolek, acoustic guitar, dulcimer
Ry Cooder: tremolo guitar
John Starling: acoustic guitar, rhythm acoustic guitar, arrangements
Herb Pedersen: banjo, vocal arrangements
Mark O'Connor: viola, fiddle, acoustic guitar, lead acoustic guitar, mandolin
Kenny Edwards: Ferrington acoustic bass, electric bass
Leland Sklar: Ferrington acoustic bass
Russ Kunkel: drums
Marty Krystall: clarinet
Brice Martin: flute
Jodi Burnett: cello
Dennis Karmazyn: cello solo
Novi Novog: viola
David Campbell: orchestrations and conductor
Charles Veal: concertmaster
Produced at The Complex (Los Angeles), Woodland (Nashville), Ocean Way (Los Angeles) between January and November 1986 by George Massenburg
Release date: 2 March 1987
Highest chart places: US: 6, UK: 60
Running time: 38:24

The stars finally aligned in 1987: Linda Ronstadt, Emmylou Harris, and Dolly Parton could finally record an album together. Their schedules worked for the effort, finally allowing the three women enough time in the studio with one another to come up with an album that met all of their standards. The recording contracts also now worked in their favor, as Dolly wasn't currently signed to a label and both Harris and Ronstadt were signed to labels that fell under the Warner Brothers conglomerate. Each woman brought songs to the others for consideration and each was given equal weight on the album, really becoming a dynamic supergroup of their own. Even back in the 1970s, the three were described as 'an indomitable combination of talent, beauty, freshness and mutual admiration' by author Mary Ellen Moore.

'Linda is such a perfectionist', Parton said in the 2019 documentary about Ronstadt's career. 'She's a pain in the ass sometimes because she is such a perfectionist. She will not have it unless it's perfect. She used to make me sing those harmonies over and over and over'. This is why having enough time to do the project right was so important; when the trio tried to make a record in the late 1970s, they rushed and didn't come up with a product that anyone was really happy with. 'We each chose favorite tracks from those sessions and incorporated them into our individual projects', Linda says in her memoir. That's how, for example, one of the songs found its way onto *Get Closer*.

The album was a resounding success for the group, reaching number six on the *Billboard* Top 200 Album chart. It did even better on the *Billboard* Top Country Albums chart, where it held the number one position for five weeks. It went up against albums by Michael Jackson, U2, Whitney Houston and Prince for the Album of the Year award at the 1988 Grammys, losing to U2. However, it did win the Grammy Award for Best Country Performance by a Duo or Group with Vocal. An enormously popular record by three superstars, it is still held in high regard and is a benchmark in the careers of all three women.

'The Pain Of Loving You' (Parton/Wagoner)

Parton takes the lead vocals on this song, which she also co-wrote. It's a good way to open the album, as it is an upbeat tune that immediately showcases the harmonizing perfection of the three members of the group. Despite playing a supportive role on this track, Ronstadt's voice is identifiable in the background as she takes the high harmony part. The subject matter of the song is the familiar territory of love gone wrong and could probably be the name for a whole genre of music inhabited solely by Linda Ronstadt tracks. Emmylou, in addition to providing part of the harmony vocals, lends acoustic guitar to the track. David Lindley's mandolin is just the right touch for this song and gives it an elevated feel due to its rare use in the country genre, lifting it from an ordinary country track to something special.

While all the women brought artistic elements to the recording sessions, longtime Ronstadt contributors Kenny Edwards and drummer Russ Kunkel lent their talents to this and many of the other tracks on the album. The consistency Ronstadt retained in her recordings, especially in the country rock realm, gave her stability in how the band would play for her. In other words, it was one less thing to worry about, as she already had a great working relationship with those playing in her band. She knew how they played and they knew how she liked them to play.

'Making Plans' (Russell/Morrison)

A slower country tune, complete with fiddle, brings to mind Ronstadt's very early albums – initially, it could be easily mistaken for one of those early tracks. Where it breaks immediately apart from that conception is when the vocals enter. For almost the first two minutes of the song, the three women sing the harmonized lead vocals together prior to Parton breaking apart to sing a verse. The way in which she is given lead vocal duties on this song, a nice surprise for listeners who expected three-part harmony for the entirety of the track, helps to underscore how rich and full their harmonies sound.

'To Know Him Is To Love Him' (Spector)
This classic rock song, originally made famous by The Teddy Bears in the 1950s, was brought in by Emmylou Harris for the group to try together, as Linda recalled in her memoir. Ronstadt's longtime manager and producer Peter Asher, had even released a version of the song in the mid-1960s when he was in a duo with Gordon Waller. A wonderfully slow ballad such as this gives the three voices room to work with one another and the listener can luxuriate in the masterful harmonies they achieve. Emmylou's vocals in the middle of the song are nothing short of angelic and the listener is drawn into her yearning as she sings about the man she loves. David Lindley, who is the only person outside of the group (and one dog) to appear in the music video, pulls double duty on this track, giving it a distinctive sound with both the mandolin and the Kona Hawaiian guitar. The latter is somewhat unusual for a country track, but it works to an impressive degree.

The music video for this song is quite charming, with the ladies gathered to make Valentines for the objects of their affection. As friends do (these friends, most definitely), they decide to take a break to sing with one another. Linda and Dolly, having more acting experience, carry more of the storyline just by utilizing their facial expressions and body language. The end of the video shows more casual moments between the women and although some of it had to be the outcome of acting, it's just as easy to believe the women had a wonderful time on the set with one another. Lindley, who is Ronstadt's cousin, also seems to have had a wonderful time playing for the three as they made paper Valentines. The video was directed by Ronstadt's fiancé at the time, George Lucas.

The magnetic charm of this song caused it to reach number one on the *Billboard* Hot Country Singles chart. It was the first single from the album and propelled its interest, as it was given over a month to become the auditory tease, persuading listeners to buy the entire album as soon as it was available.

'Hobo's Meditation' (Rodgers)
A traditional country sound meets with traditional country lyrics on this track, the first in which Linda takes lead vocals. The change in Ronstadt's voice from her early country-leaning albums up to this point is remarkable and the notes she hits on this track highlight how far her voice has progressed. The subject matter and instrumentation on the track are strikingly akin to those early albums, but Linda tackles this song and makes it a showcase of how she could do a powerful traditional country song after everyone thought she

had moved on. Herb Pedersen, who had played with Ronstadt on earlier albums, comes back to lend his expertise on the banjo. Parton and Harris pushed Ronstadt's vocals out front; while their supporting harmonies help make this song, the lead vocal from Linda marks it as something fully within her sphere. If it were not for the trained vocals Linda developed in the 1980s, this track would have been happily at home on an album such as *Prisoner In Disguise*. When the three performed on *The Tonight Show* to promote the album, this was the track they chose to highlight Linda's lead vocals.

'Wildflowers' (Parton)

Parton brought this original composition to the group for inclusion on the album. Dolly takes lead vocals on this track and uses a metaphor to tell of the desire to go where she wants to. Just as wildflowers don't care where they grow, the three women singing the song were remarkably independent and did what they wanted to do in their careers, making it a sort of anthem for them. The harmonies on this song melt together beautifully and paint a picture of wildflowers blowing in a gentle breeze. One of the most fragile songs on the album, it is situated perfectly between two songs that have very strong lead vocals from Linda. The track was the fourth and final single from the album, released over a year after the album itself, and floated to number six on the *Billboard* Hot Country Singles chart on the strength of its vocals and invoked imagery.

'Telling Me Lies' (Thompson/Cook)

Emmylou suggested this song to Ronstadt in the course of selecting tracks for the album, Linda told in her memoir, and it seems such a natural fit that it's hard to imagine her not picking it as one of her showcase songs. Longtime Ronstadt collaborator David Campbell was brought in to arrange and conduct the orchestra for this song and his touch transforms it into quite the sweeping, epic ballad. In short, it was exactly what listeners had come to expect from Linda throughout her career up until her switch to jazz standards starting in 1983.

Parton and Harris provide wonderful backup harmonies for Ronstadt as she steadily escalates her own vocals throughout the course of the song, especially in the choruses. By the end of the last chorus, Linda steamrolls over everything else involved in the track and it is, quite definitely, an instant classic. Linda's trademark scorned and hurt lyrics blast out of the speakers as the listener becomes emotionally invested. This was the second single from the album, and the first to come out after the album was released. It charted both on the *Billboard* Hot Country Singles chart and the *Billboard* Hot Adult Contemporary chart, reaching number three on the former and number 35 on the latter.

'My Dear Companion' (Ritchie)

This Emmylou-driven song gave the other two women the chance to support her with their harmonized vocals. As a showcase for Harris, it allowed her to delicately sketch the lyrics against a backdrop of acoustic instruments. A simply constructed song, it gives the listener a chance to recover from the power of 'Telling Me Lies'. Making space for an Emmylou song is important when she is in a group with Linda and Dolly; while each has a unique voice, the other two could easily be overpowering on a track such as this. However, they both scaled their harmonies back so that Harris could flourish.

'Those Memories Of You' (O'Bryant)

A thoroughly contemporary-sounding song, this was released to some degree of popularity the year prior to this album by Pam Tillis. The sound you expect from a 1980s country hit seeps off the vinyl as the album spins, giving us a shuffle beat laden with fiddle. Dolly Parton's lead vocals are wonderful on the track and her expertise at adding just the right emphasis on syllables is on full display as she croons this song in a way that only she can. The real magic touch, of course, comes when Ronstadt and Harris add their harmonies to back Parton up, making this track pop.

This song was the third single from the album and went as high as number five on the *Billboard* Hot Country Singles chart. Linda and Emmylou appeared on Dolly's television show in the same year that the album came out and chose this as one of the songs to sing together, which makes sense as Dolly has lead vocal duties. Visually, it's a treat to see them sing with one another on this show as they each wore their outfit from the album cover. This is actually the last song they sang on the program, as Emmylou sang 'My Dear Companion' and Linda sang 'Hobo's Meditation'. The way that they balanced their appearances and gave each member a chance to shine shows their respect for one another.

'I've Had Enough' (McGarrigle)

Linda chose a Kate McGarrigle song for inclusion on this album; until this point, Ronstadt had been the most mainstream artist to perform a song written by one or both of the sisters. The previous McGarrigle songs that Ronstadt had sung were all solo and she knew what to do with them; by bringing a song such as this to Parton and Harris, she trusted their creative input. David Campbell's keen experience with orchestration is obvious in the subtle, yet moving, instrument choices – including an unexpected cello solo. The way in which the three voices work together to sing this sorrowful ballad is a masterclass in harmony.

'Rosewood Casket' (traditional)

Arranged by Avie Lee Parton

Parton takes over lead vocals on this traditional track that was arranged by her own mother. Musically, it sounds close to 'Wildflowers' and brings a light, airy feeling to the album after the much heavier-sounding 'I've Had Enough'. The beautiful voices weave a story that includes the singer of the song talking about her own death. As a consequence, the track is really fleshed out and comes to life due to their sweet voices; interpreting a traditional song can give artists the opportunity to do what they want with it in order to give it a fresh sound, something Ronstadt did for three consecutive albums of jazz standards. In this way, the three women breathed new life into a song that had been around for quite a while before they sang it.

'Farther Along' (traditional)
Arranged by Emmylou Harris and John Starling
This Christian-tinged song about temptation closes out the album. The spiritual nature of the track is a fitting way to end the listener's experience – a gift from above. The whole track has shades of church woven into it, down to the use of the Hammond organ as one of the backing instruments. The track also functions as a summary of the listening experience, as each of the three is given a verse to sing lead on. In between, they come together to support one another.

Canciones de Mi Padre (1987)

Personnel:
Linda Ronstadt: vocals
Michael J. Ronstadt: vocals
Danny Valdez: vocals, guitar
Gilberto Puente: guitar
Jorge Lopez: guitar
Samuel Gutierrez: guitar
Pedro Flores: vihuela
Victor "el Pato" Cardenas: vihuela
Felipe Perez: violin
Antonio Ramos: violin
Salvador Torres: violin
Heriberto Molina: vocals
Ricardo Cisneros: vocals
Steve Fowler: flute
Ron Kalina: harmonica
Juan Gudiño: trumpet
Ignacio N Gomez: trumpet
Jim Self: tuba
Larry Bunker: percussion
Pedro Rey Jr.: vocals
Produced by Peter Asher and Ruben Fuentes
Release date: 24 November 1987
Highest chart place: US: 42
Running time: 39:41

In the fall of 2022, in an interview with the San Diego Union-Tribune, Linda Ronstadt was asked which album was her favorite. 'The Mexican music one, *Canciones de Mi Padre* (Songs for My Father)', Ronstadt answered. 'I worked really hard to make it be what I wanted it to be, which is pre-World War II ranchera music'. From an artist who is notoriously hard on herself about all her past work, it is surprising that she was able to give a definitive, firm answer.

The move to make a Mexican record was a goal Linda set for herself in the 1970s. Sprinkled throughout interviews of the era were references to a desire to make a record of mariachi music. 'But I'm just as determined to become the world's greatest Mexican singer. See, Mexican ranchera music is the equivalent of American country music', a younger Linda told *Hit Parader* in 1971. One can draw a line from 'Lo Siento mi Vida' on *Hasten Down The Wind*, to her Spanish language recording of 'Blue Bayou' in 1977, to this album. Even so, the press was surprised when this was announced as her next project. As Linda told *Vogue* in 2022, 'I'd say it in interviews all the time – 'I'm Mexican' – and it was just ignored. Like, 'You can't be Mexican. You have a German surname and you're white as a lily''.

So, what are the main musical elements in traditional mariachi music? The use of violins and horns to help punctuate the vocals of a lead singer and their backing group. The background singers typically chime in to help emphasize the overall subject of a song, or even a particular phrase, hammering home what the listener should take from hearing the song. Arguably, the most important instrument is a five-stringed acoustic guitar (known as a vihuela), with the guitar player placed very near the lead vocalist – the proximity indicating how crucial the pairing is to produce the right sound. An acoustic, fretless six-string bass guitar (known as a guitarrón) helps to round out the sound and give it rhythm.

Ronstadt took her work seriously, especially when it came to this album, and prepared in California with two groups of mariachi bands to make sure she got everything right. As the *Vogue* article explained, the mariachi field was almost all-male. However, Linda asked for assistance from the male groups to do the album the right way. 'They could have been real defensive and real schmucky, but they were completely willing to help'.

The album itself was an immediate success, going double platinum in relatively no time at all. Due to its nature as a Spanish-language album, there were no singles released. Its success, therefore, as an album with no single-related airplay, is even more impressive. Even still, it is the bestselling non-English language album in American history.

When Ronstadt toured to support the album, she had a live performance staged after how her aunt Luisa, a famous Mexican singer in her own right, had designed her own shows. The show profiled different areas of Mexico with different set pieces and costumes. Everything about Linda's outfits was custom-made by the same designer (Manuel Cuevas) who had made outfits for Johnny Cash, Elvis and The Beatles (where his work can be seen on the cover of *Sgt. Pepper's Lonely Hearts Club Band*). Still, the tour wasn't a guaranteed success: 'We would go to Dallas, say, and think, No one's coming to this arena', Ronstadt told *Vogue*. 'We went to the same venues where we played rock 'n' roll, and we had a completely different audience. And they knew the songs. They knew where to yell and scream and where to stay out of your way'. Multi-generational families would come to the show and enjoy Ronstadt's mariachi extravaganza.

In every way, this album and its tour was an astounding success which proved, once again, that Linda's musical instincts were correct. The album won the 1989 Grammy for Best Mexican-American Performance and it stands tall as one of the hallmark achievements in her career.

'Por Un Amor' (Parra)

Ronstadt opens the album with this song of lost love. As this may have been a listener's first introduction to mariachi music, Linda had to put time and thought into how she would open this world to those unfamiliar with the traditional music she so loved. The guitar and horns open the track, laying the foundation for her vocals, which she gently works into the song, letting the background singers do their job of emphasizing what she is singing about. In many ways, the subject matter of this song is a throwback to the pattern Ronstadt paved in her rock career, as it is a forlorn song of a woman who just wants to get her lost love back again. The singer longs for her life to end, as her life is nothing without her love. It's quite a dramatic song, but can really be seen (subject-wise) as similar to something like 'Poor, Poor Pitiful Me'.

The way Ronstadt delivers the song is mournful, slow and beautiful. The horns and strings weep alongside her vocals as she belts out the sad tale contained within the lyrics.

'Los Laureles' (López)

Linda's vocals start off at such a high point here and are delivered by a strong female protagonist to a man who desires her. She is able to articulate the feeling of the song strongly and with such confidence that any man who thinks of crossing her better think twice. What the singer is looking for is a commitment from her love; at its core, it's a song of a woman pursuing a man and asking him to commit to her or be gone. The mariachi music matches the feeling evoked by Ronstadt's vocals; if one wanted to pull one song from this album that epitomizes what mariachi music sounds and feels like, it is this one.

'Hay Unos Ojos' (Fuentes)

The next track is softer than the two preceding it, with Ronstadt crooning about the way her lover's eyes look. The more simple musical arrangement backing her, consisting of mariachi guitars, strikes the perfect tone as she extolls the virtues of her love. Ronstadt's vocal training comes into full play on a track such as this, as she hits high, long, powerful notes to emphasize the traditional lyrics.

In a live performance of the piece, Linda dressed in the outfit that appears on the album cover and, incredibly, delivers the song while sitting down. The ability to belt out a song like this while reclined is a mark of supreme talent. Ronstadt also performed this song with Mexican singing legend Lola Beltran, in which Beltran helped Linda interpret the song on stage for an audience of thousands. This performance predates the release of the album and Ronstadt carried a sheet of lyrics with her to reference. As far back as 1971, Linda spoke highly of Lola, telling *Hit Parader*, 'There's a singer called Lola Beltran; she's my favorite chick singer in the world... She's so good'. Linda must have been thrilled to perform with Beltran on stage, as Beltran's career coincided with Ronstadt's growing up with traditional mariachi music. 'Lola was magnificent', reflected Ronstadt. 'A tall, handsome woman with strong cheekbones, she commanded the stage, her beautiful hands moving so gracefully that they were a show in themselves'. Beltran's vocals, along with her showmanship, made a fan out of young Ronstadt years prior and the experience of performing with her live must have been something of a validation.

Beltran was supportive of Ronstadt's desire to make this record, giving her a peach-colored rebozo that Linda wore to the recording sessions. 'It gave me courage', wrote Ronstadt in her memoir. This live performance is a glimpse into how Linda developed her Spanish skills while preparing for this album; a perfectionist, Ronstadt took a risk in tackling material in a learned language.

'La Cigarra' (Pérez y Soto)
A track about a cicada's song is not something listeners would have ever heard on one of Ronstadt's English albums, but the traditional mariachi lament fits right in on this album. Ronstadt, once again, chooses a tragic song to interpret and it is similar in tone to many she had chosen before. The passion with which Linda delivers this song and the high notes she hits throughout make it a worthwhile listen. Although the lyrical subject matter is tragic, the vocals are nothing short of a celebration of traditional mariachi music, accentuated wonderfully by the backing string section. This song is so tied to Ronstadt's mariachi career that when she was given the Kennedy Center Honors in 2019, Flor de Toloache, an all-female mariachi group, sang this in tribute to her on stage. An overjoyed Ronstadt, with a giant smile on her face, applauded from the balcony as they finished the song.

'Tú Sólo Tú' (Leal)
Ronstadt is joined on vocals by a male voice, making the song seem almost like a duet – well, it would appear that way if not for Linda's powerful vocals dominating the track. However, her vocal partner helps accentuate the emotions of this song, whose title translates to 'You Only You'. The tale of the song is about a woman who drives herself to a state of ruin for the man she loves. There is footage from a performance of this song later in Ronstadt's career, in which the audience sing along with her and absolutely go wild for her interpretation of the classic ranchera song. Her obvious affection for this track for the remainder of her career is evident in this footage, as she can't help but smile as she croons the tragic lyrics and soaks up the love from the crowd.

'Y Ándale' (Elizondo)
The second song in a row to deal with a heavy-drinking protagonist, Ronstadt, nevertheless, injects a party-like atmosphere into her interpretation, which opts for a classic mariachi arrangement. 'I'm a renowned tee-totaler', Ronstadt said in the concert video produced for this song, 'but I love this drinking song'. She brought her niece Mindy to sing with her and the fun they have with one another here is obvious. The punchy strings and the men's chorus backing make this song feel jaunty and celebratory – it's a fun, expressive song to listen to and appreciate.

'Rogaciano El Huapanguero' (Trejo)
This is another journey back in time for Ronstadt, who hadn't interpreted a song that told a story in quite a long time. Here, Linda sings of a community that has lost its local performer of huapango (a traditional Mexican music and dance genre). As the song goes on, Ronstadt sings of how sad two individuals, Azucena and Cecilia, are over the loss. Even the local sugar mill is in mourning for its lost star, but Linda says, sometimes in the far-off distance, he can still be seen in the evening.

'La Charreada' (Bermejo)
A joyful brass introduction leads the listener into this celebratory, quick-paced mariachi number. Ronstadt speeds through her lines with glee; the happiness seeps in through Linda's performance and that of her backing band and vocalists. It's a song given to powerful, energetic visuals and performances. In concert, Ronstadt, backed by a semi-circle of mariachi musicians, commanded the stage and delivered the opening verse before being joined on stage by traditional dancers and a lasso artist. The atmosphere resembles the fiesta which Linda sings of in the song.

'Dos Arbolitos' (Gil)
The beauty of two trees is the inspiration behind this song, as Ronstadt sings of her desire to be with them until she dies. The versatility of mariachi music is shown in the lyrics of this track, as the genre was not wholly confined to tragic love stories. While the previous song was a celebration song, being upbeat in nature, this track slows down and dwells on the miracle of nature. In another allusion to her past (in this instance, the expectation early in her career that she was a tree-hugging hippie because she liked to wander around barefoot), this song's focus on the natural world is a delightful musically inspired change from what came before on the album.

'Corrido De Cananea' (Fuentes)
Mariachi has a way of making any lyric sound happy, with its layers of brass instruments, acoustic guitars and vocals. Ronstadt tackles this track with several fellow singers to tell a tale about being arrested and thrown into jail. The pacing of the vocals is liable to make a listener sway along with the song and soak in the beauty of the arrangement. The combined voices and the smooth instrumentation make a playful, memorable track. While the horns are present on the song, they are more subdued than they are elsewhere on the album to form a soft mariachi song.

'La Barca De Guaymas' (Fuentes)
The third and final song written by Rubén Fuentes to appear on the album (Linda drew upon his work more than any other for this album), the lyrics tell a familiar tale of doomed love. However, the way in which Ronstadt

sings the song so languidly and softly makes this pleasant to the ears of any listener. The use of strings on this track helps to evoke a sorrowful mood to match the lead vocals provided by Ronstadt. A mournful harmonica rounds out the sound of the song to make it seem lonely and sad.

'La Calandria' (Castillo)
Much like the titular lark, this track is joyful and bright and one can almost imagine flying alongside a happy lark as Linda sings about the merit of being a bird. What good is being a prideful human if your pants fall down at home? What about being a deer, when you're always in danger of being shot? Much better to be a lark and take to the sky. The musical arrangement behind Ronstadt's vocals is light and airy, making the listener want to show their wing span and live as carefree a life as the little bird. This is another happy song on the album and flits into existence as a bright penultimate track on a very full album.

'El Sol Que Tú Eres' (traditional)
Arranged by Daniel Valdez
Linda closes the album with another duet and, true to its title referencing the sun, feels like an appropriate number with which to metaphorically sunset the listening experience. A wonderfully slow number, it gives the listener one last chance to savor Ronstadt's beautiful vocals as she sings of the travails of being a poor farmer while, all the time, being accompanied by the all-seeing sun. This may be the oldest song on the album, as it is a traditional Mexican song with no writer attributes. While song order is always an important factor in constructing an album, the choice of this song as the one to close this particular album feels extremely poignant and well-planned.

Cry Like A Rainstorm, Howl Like The Wind (1989)

Personnel:
Linda Ronstadt: lead and harmony vocals, backing vocals
Aaron Neville: lead and harmony vocals
Jimmy Webb: acoustic piano, orchestral arrangements
Robbie Buchanan: keyboards, organ
Don Grolnick: acoustic piano, keyboards
William D. "Smitty" Smith: electric piano
Michael Landau: electric guitar
Dean Parks: electric guitar
Andrew Gold: electric guitar, 12-string electric guitar, guitar
Leland Sklar: bass
David Hungate: bass
Carlos Vega: drums
Russ Kunkel: drums
Michael Fisher: percussion
Peter Asher: percussion
Tower of Power: horns
Marty Paich: orchestral arrangements and conductor
Terrance Kelly: choir arrangements and conductor
David Campbell: orchestral arrangements, conductor
Greg Adams: orchestral arrangements, horn arrangements, conductor
The Skywalker Symphony Orchestra: orchestra
Pavel Farkas: concertmaster
Rosemary Butler: additional backing vocals, backing vocals
Oakland Interfaith Gospel Choir: choir
Jon Joyce: backing vocals
Arnold McCuller: backing vocals
Produced at Skywalker Ranch between March and August 1989 by Peter Asher
Release date: October 1989
Highest chart places: US: 7, UK: 43
Running time: 43:02

Linda Ronstadt returned to popular music with this album. Her experiences with jazz standards and mariachi augmented her formidable vocal talents and allowed her to return to some of her favorite writers with a much different skill set than she had prior to 1983. Linda and Peter Asher chose to make a pop album with some of her experiences guiding them, including finding a different place to record (Skywalker Sound) and employing the use of a full orchestra for much of the material on the record. In her memoir, Ronstadt described this as her best collaboration with Asher.

Ronstadt long admired Aaron Neville and was a big fan of his; seeking his collaboration for this album was a priority for her. They worked on four songs together on this album and the respect they have for one another's artistry is evident on those tracks. The album cover even gives him a credit right below her own name, highlighting Neville's significant role here. Linda's instincts, as usual, paid off. The album went triple platinum, stayed on the charts for over a year and is one of Ronstadt's three best-selling albums of all time.

The album can be seen as the culmination of Ronstadt's career to this point. While returning to some songwriters she had interpreted over the past two decades, she also applied her technical and vocal expertise in the act of bringing the songs to life. Every element of her career coalesced around this album and is a capstone experience for those who have been with Ronstadt since the beginning of her career. In that regard, it is nothing short of spectacular.

'Still Within The Sound Of My Voice' (Webb)
The first of several Jimmy Webb songs on the album, this one was originally recorded by country legend Glen Campbell two years prior to this album's release. Thus, there are two connections to Ronstadt's past already present in the song; she had previously interpreted Webb's work on *Get Closer*, and she had guested on Campbell's variety show very early in her solo career.

Webb himself contributes piano to the track and lends the songwriter's touch. Ronstadt's vocals are crystal clear and build up this epic of a song, inviting the listener to be swept up in the drama of the track as it constructs a reality unto itself. Ronstadt leverages her experience from the past decade, including operetta and American standards, to control her vocals and let them burst out when demanded by the song. Should listeners be unaware of her work since her last pop album seven years prior, this song introduces Linda's heightened skills as a singer and arranger.

'As a songwriter, Jimmy Webb kills me', Linda reflected in her memoir, 'His songs are difficult, but the emotional dividend is worth the risk a singer must take in scaling the tremendous melodic range his compositions explore'.

'Cry Like A Rainstorm' (Kaz)
Another familiar writer, Eric Kaz, supplied this song for the next track on the album. Similar to other Kaz songs covered by Ronstadt, this one is introspective and gives Linda wonderful lyrics and imagery to play with as she works with Rosemary Butler and a full choir to deliver this song. The album took its name from this track, which makes sense, as the song makes a clear statement on the mood of the album. The undercurrent of passion on this track – with its gripping vocals and immaculate instrumental production – and the overall album, brings to mind the type of songs Ronstadt was best known for in the 1970s, such as 'You're No Good', 'Heart Like A Wheel' and 'Blue Bayou'.

Terrance Kelly's choral direction is crucial in making the choir blend so well with Ronstadt's lead vocals without becoming overpowering. This is the first time Linda worked with a full choir for background support on an album and it is truly interesting to see how she utilized them as a way to augment a track such as this. The choir make the song feel full and add a depth that would have been lacking should they not have been included.

'All My Life' (Bonoff)
In another welcome return, Ronstadt turned to Karla Bonoff for this and two other songs on the album. Bonoff's work had been a fixture of ***Hasten Down The Wind*** and the material she continued to produce drew Linda's attention. While this song was originally recorded by Karla a year prior to this album's release, the combination of Ronstadt and Aaron Neville on this track made it a smash success. It went to number 11 on the *Billboard* Hot 100 and number one on the *Billboard* Adult Contemporary chart. At the 1991 Grammys, it was awarded Best Pop Performance by a Duo or Group with Vocal.

The blend of Linda and Aaron's voices belies the admiration they had for one another and how their mutual respect and artisanship made their tracks seem like a natural extension of both their careers, rather than something out of the ordinary. Linda's keen instinct for recognizing a song's potential and then working it into her style and vision was in full force on a song like this. Another blast from the past is present on this track, as Andrew Gold plays an effective electric guitar part. David Campbell, the longtime orchestral arranger and conductor from early in Ronstadt's career, lends his touch to the album for the first time on this track. Although the sound of the song is very fresh, the classic touches from longtime friends and collaborators also make the song feel simultaneously comfortable and familiar.

'I Need You' (Carrack/Lowe/Belmont)
This track sounds like it could have been included on one of Ronstadt's albums in the 1970s in the midst of her rock heyday. It's classic Linda through and through and is made even better by the inclusion of Neville for her to play off. They trade lines in the song in a playful manner and sing the lyrics with sincerity. Ronstadt's vocals are precise and powerful and are reminiscent of her work on standards. Given a different arrangement, this song could masquerade as one from the Great American Songbook rather than one written in the early 1980s. With just a couple of male backup singers and light strings applied, this upbeat track is well-placed on the album at this juncture.

'Don't Know Much' (Mann/Weil/Snow)
Perhaps the best-known track from this album (although 'All My Life' may also lay claim to that title), this song is the epitome of Ronstadt and Neville's cohesiveness as a vocal duo. The song was released three times in the nine years before this album, once by one of the co-writers of the song, Barry Mann, and then by Bill Medley and Bette Midler. Once again, Linda chose a song sung by a singular artist and transformed it into a duet.

The focal point is the almost perfect vocals by both Linda and Aaron. They build off one another to drive the song to a truly extraordinary place and speak to Ronstadt's keen ability to tune into another artist's style and mold her voice to it, thus making the overall product better than its separate parts. As this was the lead single from the album, a music video was shot and really leans into the intimate nature of the song and the close working relationship between the two, coloring it as a romance for the sake of the video's storyline.

The song reached the top spot on the *Billboard* Adult Contemporary chart and hit the Top Ten of the *Billboard* Hot 100. This is the last Linda Ronstadt song to chart; it also just missed out on being a platinum single, instead settling for gold status at over 900,000 copies sold in the United States. It also won the 1990 Grammy for Best Pop Vocal Performance by a Duo or Group.

'Adios' (Webb)

Guest musician – Brian Wilson: backing vocals, arrangements

A Jimmy Webb song opened the first side of the album and another now closes it. The Beach Boys' founding member Brian Wilson not only sang backup on this track but also completed the arrangement for it. Having someone many consider a master of pop music lend his touch to an album is a high compliment and speaks to the respect that the industry had for her. Wilson's technical prowess is on display here through his use of harmonized vocals as a backdrop to Ronstadt's lead, giving the listener a ghost of a Beach Boys feeling. 'In the studio, under Brian's direction, we recorded his harmony parts', Linda wrote in her memoir, 'with five separate tracks of unison singing on each of the three parts, 15 vocal tracks in all... the creamy vocal smoothness instantly recognizable as The Beach Boys'.

The California feeling of the song, as mentioned in the lyrics and evoked by the arrangement, combines with the feeling of lost love to provide a summation of so many threads from throughout her career. Linda's vocals sound wickedly close to those she recorded a decade and a half prior, really making this whole song feel like a cozy throwback that would fit in on any of her albums from 1974 through to 1982. It's a beautiful callback and is the perfect way to end side one.

'Trouble Again' (Bonoff/Edwards)

The second half of the album opens with this great rock song that brings to mind many from the 1980s. It's a fun way to see how Linda had evolved her rock sensibilities. This Karla Bonoff and Kenny Edwards song gave Ronstadt plenty to work with, especially considering her relationship with the two writers. Andrew Gold is back for this track, as is Ronstadt's rock drummer Russ Kunkel. Peter Asher even takes on percussion duties here, making it a bit of a reunion for Ronstadt and her bandmates.

The way in which this track differs from her classic rock offerings is a hallmark of this album and signposts it as something special to this part of her career: string arrangements back everything and Ronstadt's ability to hold a strong note is a marked difference from her earlier efforts. This track is a wonderful marriage of the old and new.

'I Keep It Hid' (Webb)
This is the third Jimmy Webb song on the album and, as such, is another piano-driven track that slowly opens up. Much like Webb's 'The Moon Is A Harsh Mistress' from *Get Closer*, it gives Linda the chance to powerfully blast out the lyrics. The result is mesmerizing, with Ronstadt giving a commanding performance. The ballad is familiar territory and yet, no matter how often she turned to them in her career, each one felt unique and special in their own right. The versatility of her vision and interpretation is the key to Ronstadt keeping her material fresh and retaining the listener's attention.

The application of the choir near the end of the song is production mastery at its best. If there was any more of it on the track, it would detract from the overall focus on Linda's voice. If it wasn't there, the song would ring a bit hollow. But injected as it was, it gives the track just the right amount of boldness that carries it from ordinary to exceptional.

'So Right, So Wrong' (Carrack/Lowe/Belmont/Ceiling/Eller)
This song, similar to the one before, is pure 1980s rock fun. An effective instrumental arrangement leads us to Ronstadt's vocals. The choir provide subtle backing for Linda as she tells the listener about her attraction to a man she randomly encounters. The choir repeat Linda's lines along the way and help buoy the song as a singalong number to loosen up anyone who, at this point, may have been stoically listening to the record. It also helps set the beginning of this side of the album apart from the ballad-heavy first side. This is another hallmark of Ronstadt's career shining through; the balance of a record is an exact science and she and Asher provide their magic once again here.

'Shattered' (Webb)
On the topic of balancing the album, or even this side of the album, Ronstadt decided to include one last Webb composition to shift the mood from the previous song to a lower-key vibe here. Another piano-driven ballad for Linda to exercise her voice with, she sings a sad lament about a broken relationship. Although the full orchestra does get a chance to interject near the end of the song, it remains a straightforward ballad that is pretty and simple at its core.

'When Something Is Wrong with My Baby' (Hayes/Porter)
Aaron Neville returns for his fourth and final appearance as he and Linda take this tune for a spin. Neville's vocals lead off the track as his emotions spill over onto the vinyl. The way in which he delivers his vocals is pristine

and he sounds exactly as he did at the height of his popularity with his brother in the 1960s. Linda slices in with her own vocals and they conspire with Neville's to drive the track to excellence. The tinkling piano and the horns behind the vocals make it feel like a Motown record. This song, just like 'Adios', could be transported back in time 25 years and feel like it totally belonged. The song was a minor chart hit, rising to number 78 on the *Billboard* Hot 100 in 1990.

The night after winning the Grammy for 'Don't Know Much', Ronstadt and Neville appeared on *The Tonight Show* to perform this song. The energy they both brought to the stage in Los Angeles is evident and their joy in being able to sing with one another can be seen. The horns are present for this live version – after all, it wouldn't be the great song it is without them. Kunkel on drums and Gold on guitar complete the throwback sound of the song and make it a special piece to watch, as the magic Linda and Aaron laid down on vinyl comes to life before the viewer's eyes.

'Goodbye My Friend' (Bonoff)

Much like Webb on side one, Karla Bonoff compositions open and close this side of the record. Ronstadt's rock band join her on this closing track. The slower tempo is a good way in which to close the album and is a fitting way for the listener to bid goodbye to Linda, and for her to return the favor with some gorgeous vocals that tug at the heartstrings. It's a bittersweet way to leave the first two decades of Ronstadt's solo career, but gives the listener the opportunity to pause and appreciate what Linda is singing directly to them. Like her, we will be okay.

Bonus Track

'Somewhere Out There' (Horner/Mann/Weil)

Although released two years prior to this album, thematically, it belongs alongside this album as it heralded Linda Ronstadt's return to popular music. Recorded as the theme for the animated movie *American Tail*, it was a duet recorded between Ronstadt and James Ingram. The film's producer, Steven Spielberg, recruited the two singers to interpret the song he had commissioned for the film. The song features many of the things featured on this album, including sweeping orchestration and dynamic, powerful vocals. It's a joy to listen to and is one of those songs that will remain in a listener's head for weeks after hearing it.

The love song, sung as a romantic ballad by the duo, was a smash hit. The infectious nature of the song boosted it to the Top Ten in the United States, the United Kingdom, Canada and Ireland. It also earned Ronstadt and Ingram the Grammy for Song of the Year, as well as Best Song Written Specifically for a Motion Picture or Television. It is also the closest Ronstadt came to winning an Academy Award, as it was nominated for Best Original Song (it lost to 'Take My Breath Away' from *Top Gun*).

Bibliography

Author not known, 'Deep Dive: Linda Ronstadt, Get Closer' (Rhino Records Website, 15 July 2020)

Author not known, 'Linda Down the Wind' (*Time*, 28 February 1977)

Author not known, 'Linda Ronstadt: An Exclusive Interview' (*Country Song Roundup*, October 1970)

Author not known, 'Ronstadt Interview – First London Concert' (*The Guardian*, 12 November 1976)

Author not known, 'September 1978: Linda Ronstadt Releases Living in the USA' (Rhino Records Website, 19 September 2022)

Author not known, 'The Styles of Linda Ronstadt' (*Rolling Stone*, 3 April 1980)

Author not known, 'Single Stories: Linda Ronstadt, Love is a Rose' (Rhino Records Website, 19 August 2022)

Aguirre, A., 'Linda Ronstadt on Her New Memoir, Feels Like Home, and Her Mexican American Heritage' (*Vogue*, 28 September 2022)

Amburn, E., *Dark Star: The Roy Orbison Story* (Carol Publishing Group, 1990)

Arrington, C., 'Oreos and Love Gone Wrong: A Heart To Heart with Linda Ronstadt' (*Creem Magazine*, December 1976)

Beland, J. *Best Seat in the House* (John Beland Productions Publisher, 2018)

Coppage, N., 'Linda Ronstadt' (*Stereo Review*, November 1976)

Crowe, C., 'Linda Ronstadt: The Million-Dollar Woman' (*Rolling Stone*, 2 December 1976)

Everett, T., '"Heat Wave": The Long Hot Sessions' (*Rolling Stone*, 18 December 1975)

Flans, R., 'The Mix Interview: Linda Ronstadt' (*Mix Online*, 15 April 2020)

Fong-Torres, B., 'Linda Ronstadt: Heartbreak on Wheels' (*Rolling Stone*, 27 March 1975)

Hamill, P., 'Linda Ronstadt, Pirate Queen' (*New York Magazine*, 21 July 1980)

Hart, R., 'Linda Ronstadt & Collaborators Look Back on 'Mad Love' at 40' (*Billboard*, 10 March 2020)

Herbst, P., 'Rock's Venus Takes Control of Her Affairs' (*Rolling Stone*, 19 October 1978)

Hilburn, R., 'Ronstadt Marching to a Different Drum' (*Deseret News*, 14 December 1993)

Hurwitz, M., 'Classic Track: 'You're No Good', Linda Ronstadt' (*Mix Online*, 5 November 2014)

Jefferson, M., Smith, S., 'Out of Disguise' (*Newsweek*, 20 October 1975)

Kahliss, J., 'Alta Q&A: "Heart Like A Wheel"' (*Alta Journal*, 25 September 2023)

Knobler, P., 'Linda Ronstadt: It's Not That Easy Being the Pretty Girl on the Block' (*Crawdaddy Magazine*, June 1974)

Mehler, M., 'Ronstadt Reigns: Linda's Happier Now, and Her New LP's Not the Only Reason Why' (*Circus Magazine*, 31 October 1978)

Moore, M., *Linda Ronstadt Scrapbook* (Ace Books, 1978)
Morris, P., 'Linda Ronstadt: Can a Sow Lover Make a Silk Purse Out of a Record Album?' (*Circus Magazine*, May 1970)
Newton, J., *Man of Tomorrow: The Relentless Life of Jerry Brown* (Little, Brown 2020)
Orloff, K., *Rock'n Roll Woman* (Nash, 1974)
Robinson, L., 'Linda Ronstadt: The Hit Parader Interview – Part 2' (*Hit Parader Magazine*, May 1978)
Rockwell, J., 'Linda Ronstadt: Her Soft-Core Charms' (*New Times*, 14 October 1977)
Rockwell, J., *Living in the USA from Stranded – Rock and Roll for a Desert Island* (Da Capo Press, 1978)
Ronstadt, L., *Simple Dreams: A Musical Memoir* (Simon & Schuster, 2013)
Rosenbaum, R., 'Melancholy Baby' (*Esquire*, October 1985)
Rubenstein, S., 'Linda Ronstadt: Superstar in Disguise' (*Circus Magazine*, 30 December 1975)
Screiberg, S., 'Linda Ronstadt: To the Beat of a Different Drum' (*USA Weekend*, 28 November 1986)
Schruers, F., 'Linda Ronstadt Walks the Plank' (*New York Sunday News*, 3 August 1980)
Senoff, P., 'Female Rocker Roundup' (*Fusion*, 26 December 1969)
Senoff, P., 'Linda Ronstadt: Sanity on the Line Every Show' (*Hit Parader Magazine*, February 1971)
Tobler, J., 'Linda Ronstadt: The West Coast's First Lady of Country-Rock' (*Country Music People*, December 1977)
Varga, G., 'Linda Ronstadt Bonus Q&A' (*The San Diego Union-Tribune*, September 23, 2022)
Windeler, R., 'When Will She Be Loved: Linda Ronstadt Finds the Time, At Last, Is Now' (*People*, 17 November 1975)

On Track series

Allman Brothers Band – Andrew Wild 978-1-78952-252-5
Tori Amos – Lisa Torem 978-1-78952-142-9
Aphex Twin – Beau Waddell 978-1-78952-267-9
Asia – Peter Braidis 978-1-78952-099-6
Badfinger – Robert Day-Webb 978-1-878952-176-4
Barclay James Harvest – Keith and Monica Domone 978-1-78952-067-5
Beck – Arthur Lizie 978-1-78952-258-7
The Beatles – Andrew Wild 978-1-78952-009-5
The Beatles Solo 1969-1980 – Andrew Wild 978-1-78952-030-9
Blue Oyster Cult – Jacob Holm-Lupo 978-1-78952-007-1
Blur – Matt Bishop 978-178952-164-1
Marc Bolan and T.Rex – Peter Gallagher 978-1-78952-124-5
Kate Bush – Bill Thomas 978-1-78952-097-2
Camel – Hamish Kuzminski 978-1-78952-040-8
Captain Beefheart – Opher Goodwin 978-1-78952-235-8
Caravan – Andy Boot 978-1-78952-127-6
Cardiacs – Eric Benac 978-1-78952-131-3
Nick Cave and The Bad Seeds – Dominic Sanderson 978-1-78952-240-2
Eric Clapton Solo – Andrew Wild 978-1-78952-141-2
The Clash – Nick Assirati 978-1-78952-077-4
Elvis Costello and The Attractions – Georg Purvis 978-1-78952-129-0
Crosby, Stills and Nash – Andrew Wild 978-1-78952-039-2
Creedence Clearwater Revival – Tony Thompson 978-178952-237-2
The Damned – Morgan Brown 978-1-78952-136-8
Deep Purple and Rainbow 1968-79 – Steve Pilkington 978-1-78952-002-6
Dire Straits – Andrew Wild 978-1-78952-044-6
The Doors – Tony Thompson 978-1-78952-137-5
Dream Theater – Jordan Blum 978-1-78952-050-7
Eagles – John Van der Kiste 978-1-78952-260-0
Earth, Wind and Fire – Bud Wilkins 978-1-78952-272-3
Electric Light Orchestra – Barry Delve 978-1-78952-152-8
Emerson Lake and Palmer – Mike Goode 978-1-78952-000-2
Fairport Convention – Kevan Furbank 978-1-78952-051-4
Peter Gabriel – Graeme Scarfe 978-1-78952-138-2
Genesis – Stuart MacFarlane 978-1-78952-005-7
Gentle Giant – Gary Steel 978-1-78952-058-3
Gong – Kevan Furbank 978-1-78952-082-8
Green Day – William E. Spevack 978-1-78952-261-7
Hall and Oates – Ian Abrahams 978-1-78952-167-2
Hawkwind – Duncan Harris 978-1-78952-052-1
Peter Hammill – Richard Rees Jones 978-1-78952-163-4
Roy Harper – Opher Goodwin 978-1-78952-130-6
Jimi Hendrix – Emma Stott 978-1-78952-175-7
The Hollies – Andrew Darlington 978-1-78952-159-7
Horslips – Richard James 978-1-78952-263-1
The Human League and The Sheffield Scene – Andrew Darlington 978-1-78952-186-3
The Incredible String Band – Tim Moon 978-1-78952-107-8
Iron Maiden – Steve Pilkington 978-1-78952-061-3
Joe Jackson – Richard James 978-1-78952-189-4
Jefferson Airplane – Richard Butterworth 978-1-78952-143-6
Jethro Tull – Jordan Blum 978-1-78952-016-3
Elton John in the 1970s – Peter Kearns 978-1-78952-034-7
Billy Joel – Lisa Torem 978-1-78952-183-2
Judas Priest – John Tucker 978-1-78952-018-7
Kansas – Kevin Cummings 978-1-78952-057-6
The Kinks – Martin Hutchinson 978-1-78952-172-6
Korn – Matt Karpe 978-1-78952-153-5
Led Zeppelin – Steve Pilkington 978-1-78952-151-1
Level 42 – Matt Philips 978-1-78952-102-3
Little Feat – Georg Purvis - 978-1-78952-168-9
Aimee Mann – Jez Rowden 978-1-78952-036-1
Joni Mitchell – Peter Kearns 978-1-78952-081-1
The Moody Blues – Geoffrey Feakes 978-1-78952-042-2
Motorhead – Duncan Harris 978-1-78952-173-3
Nektar – Scott Meze – 978-1-78952-257-0
New Order – Dennis Remmer – 978-1-78952-249-5
Nightwish – Simon McMurdo – 978-1-78952-270-9
Laura Nyro – Philip Ward 978-1-78952-182-5
Mike Oldfield – Ryan Yard 978-1-78952-060-6
Opeth – Jordan Blum 978-1-78-952-166-5
Pearl Jam – Ben L. Connor 978-1-78952-188-7
Tom Petty – Richard James 978-1-78952-128-3
Pink Floyd – Richard Butterworth 978-1-78952-242-6
The Police – Pete Braidis 978-1-78952-158-0
Porcupine Tree – Nick Holmes 978-1-78952-144-3
Queen – Andrew Wild 978-1-78952-003-3
Radiohead – William Allen 978-1-78952-149-8
Rancid – Paul Matts 989-1-78952-187-0
Renaissance – David Detmer 978-1-78952-062-0
REO Speedwagon – Jim Romag 978-1-78952-262-4
The Rolling Stones 1963-80 – Steve Pilkington 978-1-78952-017-0
The Smiths and Morrissey – Tommy Gunnarsson 978-1-78952-140-5
Spirit – Rev. Keith A. Gordon – 978-1-78952- 248-8
Stackridge – Alan Draper 978-1-78952-232-7
Status Quo the Frantic Four Years – Richard James 978-1-78952-160-3
Steely Dan – Jez Rowden 978-1-78952-043-9
Steve Hackett – Geoffrey Feakes 978-1-78952-098-9
Tears For Fears – Paul Clark - 978-178952-238-9
Thin Lizzy – Graeme Stroud 978-1-78952-064-4

Tool – Matt Karpe 978-1-78952-234-1
Toto – Jacob Holm-Lupo 978-1-78952-019-4
U2 – Eoghan Lyng 978-1-78952-078-1
UFO – Richard James 978-1-78952-073-6
Van Der Graaf Generator – Dan Coffey 978-1-78952-031-6
Van Halen – Morgan Brown – 9781-78952-256-3
The Who – Geoffrey Feakes 978-1-78952-076-7
Roy Wood and the Move – James R Turner 978-1-78952-008-8
Yes – Stephen Lambe 978-1-78952-001-9
Frank Zappa 1966 to 1979 – Eric Benac 978-1-78952-033-0
Warren Zevon – Peter Gallagher 978-1-78952-170-2
10CC – Peter Kearns 978-1-78952-054-5

Decades Series

The Bee Gees in the 1960s – Andrew Mon Hughes et al 978-1-78952-148-1
The Bee Gees in the 1970s – Andrew Mon Hughes et al 978-1-78952-179-5
Black Sabbath in the 1970s – Chris Sutton 978-1-78952-171-9
Britpop – Peter Richard Adams and Matt Pooler 978-1-78952-169-6
Phil Collins in the 1980s – Andrew Wild 978-1-78952-185-6
Alice Cooper in the 1970s – Chris Sutton 978-1-78952-104-7
Alice Cooper in the 1980s – Chris Sutton 978-1-78952-259-4
Curved Air in the 1970s – Laura Shenton 978-1-78952-069-9
Donovan in the 1960s – Jeff Fitzgerald 978-1-78952-233-4
Bob Dylan in the 1980s – Don Klees 978-1-78952-157-3
Brian Eno in the 1970s – Gary Parsons 978-1-78952-239-6
Faith No More in the 1990s – Matt Karpe 978-1-78952-250-1
Fleetwood Mac in the 1970s – Andrew Wild 978-1-78952-105-4
Fleetwood Mac in the 1980s – Don Klees 978-178952-254-9
Focus in the 1970s – Stephen Lambe 978-1-78952-079-8
Free and Bad Company in the 1970s – John Van der Kiste 978-1-78952-178-8
Genesis in the 1970s – Bill Thomas 978178952-146-7
George Harrison in the 1970s – Eoghan Lyng 978-1-78952-174-0
Kiss in the 1970s – Peter Gallagher 978-1-78952-246-4
Manfred Mann's Earth Band in the 1970s – John Van der Kiste 978178952-243-3
Marillion in the 1980s – Nathaniel Webb 978-1-78952-065-1
Van Morrison in the 1970s – Peter Childs - 978-1-78952-241-9
Mott the Hoople and Ian Hunter in the 1970s – John Van der Kiste 978-1-78-952-162-7
Pink Floyd In The 1970s – Georg Purvis 978-1-78952-072-9
Suzi Quatro in the 1970s – Darren Johnson 978-1-78952-236-5
Queen in the 1970s – James Griffiths 978-1-78952-265-5
Roxy Music in the 1970s – Dave Thompson 978-1-78952-180-1
Slade in the 1970s – Darren Johnson 978-1-78952-268-6
Status Quo in the 1980s – Greg Harper 978-1-78952-244-0
Tangerine Dream in the 1970s – Stephen Palmer 978-1-78952-161-0
The Sweet in the 1970s – Darren Johnson 978-1-78952-139-9
Uriah Heep in the 1970s – Steve Pilkington 978-1-78952-103-0
Van der Graaf Generator in the 1970s – Steve Pilkington 978-1-78952-245-7
Rick Wakeman in the 1970s – Geoffrey Feakes 978-1-78952-264-8
Yes in the 1980s – Stephen Lambe with David Watkinson 978-1-78952-125-2

Other Books

1967: A Year In Psychedelic Rock 978-1-78952-155-9
1970: A Year In Rock – John Van der Kiste 978-1-78952-147-4
1973: The Golden Year of Progressive Rock 978-1-78952-165-8
Babysitting A Band On The Rocks – G.D. Praetorius 978-1-78952-106-1
Eric Clapton Sessions – Andrew Wild 978-1-78952-177-1
Derek Taylor: For Your Radioactive Children – Andrew Darlington 978-1-78952-038-5
The Golden Road: The Recording History of The Grateful Dead – John Kilbride 978-1-78952-156-6
Iggy and The Stooges On Stage 1967-1974 – Per Nilsen 978-1-78952-101-6
Jon Anderson and the Warriors – the road to Yes – David Watkinson 978-1-78952-059-0
Magic: The David Paton Story – David Paton 978-1-78952-266-2
Misty: The Music of Johnny Mathis – Jakob Baekgaard 978-1-78952-247-1
Nu Metal: A Definitive Guide – Matt Karpe 978-1-78952-063-7
Tommy Bolin: In and Out of Deep Purple – Laura Shenton 978-1-78952-070-5
Maximum Darkness – Deke Leonard 978-1-78952-048-4
The Twang Dynasty – Deke Leonard 978-1-78952-049-1

and many more to come!